The Untold Experiences of a Navy Corpsman

THE UNTOLD EXPERIENCES OF A NAVY CORPSMAN

A US Navy Hospital Corpsman with a US Marine Corps Reconnaissance Patrol Team in the 1950's on covert Korean missions.

Written by

C. Gilbert Lowery

United States Navy Hospital Corpsman
United States Marine Corps Corpsman

authorHOUSE®

AuthorHouse™
1663 Liberty Drive
Bloomington, IN 47403
www.authorhouse.com
Phone: 1-800-839-8640

© *2011 C. Gilbert Lowery. All rights reserved.*

No part of this book may be reproduced, stored in a retrieval system, or transmitted by any means without the written permission of the author.

First published by AuthorHouse 5/2/2011

ISBN: 978-1-4567-3161-8 (e)
ISBN: 978-1-4567-3162-5 (hc)
ISBN: 978-1-4567-3163-2 (sc)

Library of Congress Control Number: 2011906058

Printed in the United States of America

Any people depicted in stock imagery provided by Thinkstock are models, and such images are being used for illustrative purposes only. Certain stock imagery © *Thinkstock.*

This book is printed on acid-free paper.

Because of the dynamic nature of the Internet, any web addresses or links contained in this book may have changed since publication and may no longer be valid. The views expressed in this work are solely those of the author and do not necessarily reflect the views of the publisher, and the publisher hereby disclaims any responsibility for them.

Dedication

This book is dedicated first to Master Chief Hospital Corpsman William Richard Charette. Master Chief Charette is a Medal of Honor recipient for his heroic actions during the Korean War. He was one of the instructors and role models in my training as a hospital corpsman at Great Lakes Naval Hospital Corps School.

I further dedicate this book to the current and former corpsmen and medics from all our military branches, including the US Navy and Marine Corps, the US Army, the US Air Force, and the US Coast Guard.

And I proudly dedicate my work to my wife, Carol, and to my family, who have supported me through many struggles and successes. I am truly blessed.

"I'm The One Called Doc"

I shall not walk in your footsteps,
but I will walk by your side.
I shall not walk in your image;
I've earned my own title of pride.
We've answered the call together,
on sea and foreign land.
When the cry for help was given,
I've been there right at hand.
Whether I am on the ocean
or in the jungle wearing greens,
Giving aid to my fellow man,
be it sailors or marines.
So the next time you see a corpsman
And you think of calling him "squid,"
think of the job he's doing
as those before him did.
And if you ever have to go out there
and your life is on the block,
Look at the one right next to you …
I'm the one called "Doc."

—*Harry D. Penny, Jr. HMC(AC)USN © 1975*
Reprinted with permission of the author.

Table of Contents

Preface		ix
Chapter 1	Pyonggang Airfield	1
Chapter 2	Kaesong	29
Chapter 3	Sariwon	49
Chapter 4	Pyongyang	69
Chapter 5	Rest and Relaxation	89
Chapter 6	Rehabilitation	101
Chapter 7	Back to Sea	113
Chapter 8	Return to Sariwon	137
Chapter 9	Back to Sea—Again	163

Preface

This story depicts my previously untold experiences as a hospital corpsman in the US Navy serving at Great Lakes Naval Hospital in Illinois and at Camp LeJeune Naval Hospital in North Carolina, aboard the USS *General A. E. Anderson* (TAP 111) and the USS *General D. I. Sultan* (TAP120)—both were military sea transport service troop ships out of Fort Mason, San Francisco, California. It then goes on to cover the events I experienced while assigned as medical support with a US Marine Corps Reconnaissance Patrol Team in Korea in the mid-1950s. I served on active duty from September 1954 until September 1958 and in the Navy Reserves from September 1958 until my Honorable Discharge in September 1962. While the names used in the book are fictitious, the facts and timeframe are true to the best of my recollection. I used the assumed name of Lawrence "Larry" Gentry in the story which was the name assigned to me by the Marine Reconnaissance Patrol Team while on the covert missions.

A cease fire and a stoppage of military conflict occurred on July 27, 1953, when an armistice agreement was signed establishing a demilitarized zone following the Panmunjom Peace Talks. However, no peace treaty has been signed to date, technically leaving North and South Korea still at war. The Communists finally agreed to accept a United Nations proposal to exchange sick and wounded prisoners. Approximately 480,000 US troops fought in the Korean War, with 36,940 killed, 103,000 wounded, 8,142 missing in action (MIA), and 3,746 taken as prisoners of war (POW). North Korea lost 215,000 troops, and China lost 114,000 troops. There may still be American and other allied troops being held captive in North Korea and China.

Following each of the five missions into North Korea, we were immediately debriefed and each of us was required to sign a statement declaring he would not reveal any details of the actions we had been involved in or where we had traveled to. Each of us held Top Secret Clearance for "Sensitive Compartmented Information." For ten years following my separation from active military service in 1958, two CIA or Secret Service agents visited me once a year to ascertain I had not revealed any information concerning the secret missions and reminded me of my oath of secrecy. I have heard nothing from any branch of our government since their last visit in 1969.

Chapter 1

Pyonggang Airfield

The sound of the helicopter blades thumping through the cool, night air was the only sound louder than my heart pounding in my chest. We were flying low to stay under the radar stations along the North Korean coastline. The two helicopters flew inland to the drop point just five miles north of Pyonggang Airfield; the lieutenant was giving last-minute instructions to the reconnaissance team members on ours. The gunnery sergeant on our sister helicopter was doing the same to his men. Well after midnight, it was now thirty minutes to our drop point.

There were twelve members in the reconnaissance team, with nine US Marines, one US Navy hospital corpsman, and two South Korean army soldiers who acted as guides and translators. As the only corpsman, or medic, on this team, I was the only one who had not been on one of these missions before.

We were flying into North Korea under the cover of darkness to identify, document, and when possible, destroy ammunition dumps and anti-aircraft gun emplacements and to document troop numbers and locations. The target locations were identified in aerial photographs taken by our U-2 spy planes, which flew weekly missions throughout and after the Korean War.

Suddenly, the small, yellow lights began flashing beside each side door, indicating we were near our target. The helicopter crew chief released ropes out each of the doors, on which we would rappel to the ground from the two airships.

"When the green light flashes, you gentlemen have thirty seconds to disembark," bellowed the pilot over the intercom. "Make it snappy. I have to get back to the carrier for a hot shower and a hot meal!"

"Thanks a lot," I remember thinking. Then the green light flashed on and Corporal Johnson punched me in the arm and said, "I'll go first, and as soon as my helmet drops below the skid, you follow me. And remember that Lieutenant Skinner will be right behind you."

The late February air from the downdraft was colder and harsher than I had expected. The rope slid rapidly through my hands as I rappelled fifty feet to the uneven, rocky ground. Corporal Johnson grabbed me and pulled me aside just as the lieutenant hit the ground, hard.

Just as quickly as we arrived, the helicopters were gone, and the cold night seemed awfully quiet after the hour and a half on the noisy, drafty chopper. Lieutenant Skinner called me over to check his foot. He had landed on a rock with his right foot and turned his ankle. After examining him, I determined he had sprained his ankle; he was in quite a bit of pain, needless to say. Gunnery Sergeant Potter came over and asked, "Are we going to have to shoot the SOB? Back home on the farm if a horse or cow broke his leg we'd just shoot 'em."

I replied, "I don't think so, Gunny. His foot doesn't appear to be broken. I'll patch him up, give him a shot, and get him going."

"Thanks a lot, Gunny. I'll remember that," replied the lieutenant.

"But right now, the first thing we need to do is get to cover in that line of trees over there and then do what you gotta do," whispered Gunny. "If you look down the hill at those lights, we have company coming."

No sooner had we scrambled behind the trees than a group of eight to ten North Korean soldiers with flashlights came up the hill to our drop area and spread out, looking for us. We stayed low behind the trees and rocks. I'll bet I was lower to the ground than anyone else. Our team was spread out ten to twenty feet back into the trees, and three of the North Korean soldiers were getting closer and closer. At once, the three soldiers were taken out, silently, by the marines. Our two South Korean soldiers, Sergeant Kwan and Corporal Park, picked up the flashlights, moved downhill from our location, and called the remaining North Korean soldiers to them as if they were their comrades. On signal, Kwan and Park hit the ground as the enemy soldiers approached, and we opened fire, killing them all in a matter of seconds.

It was time to move out. We pulled the dead soldiers back into the trees and out of the line of sight. We searched them for maps and other useful information, and then disabled and tossed their weapons deeper into the woods

We moved out as fast as we could after making all that ruckus. We took turns helping Lieutenant Skinner as he hobbled on his sprained ankle. It was dark, but Sergeant Kwan knew the landscape well—we were only about ten miles from where he'd been born and raised. His family had escaped to South Korea in 1949, and he'd immediately joined the South Korean army. The time was now 0315, and we had still to travel five miles before daylight caught us in the open.

At 0430, we stopped for a breather and a drink of water. Corporal Park came over to me and whispered, "Hey, Doc. Take a look at my arm. I think I got a little scratch back there in that skirmish." I pulled up his sleeve, and he had a cut about four inches long on his forearm. He had wrapped a handkerchief around it and said nothing to anyone. I cleaned the wound, closed it with eighteen to twenty stitches, applied sulfa powder—the antibacterial of choice before penicillin—and bandaged his arm. He didn't want anyone to know he had been injured.

Lieutenant Skinner signaled for us to move out. While we'd been stopped, the gunnery sergeant had found a forked tree branch and fashioned a crutch for the lieutenant, which made it easier for him to get around by himself. Sergeant Kwan then took the lead, since he knew where we were headed. Corporal Park and Private Finch brought up the rear. We moved along single file for the most part, heading west toward our first objective. We did not use lights for obvious reasons, and the going was slow and deliberate. We could hear vehicles moving to our north.

We had climbed over one hill and around another when Kwan started up one more hill, just as the first sign of daylight was approaching. He signaled with his left arm to stop and stay low. We heard footsteps coming our way, as if two or more people were running. We hid in the underbrush, and three young men ran by us and down the hill. Two of them were carrying chickens. It was all we could do to keep from laughing out loud, thinking they were teenagers stealing food for their families. It shows why you don't shoot first before you know what is happening. We skirted around a group of shacks halfway up the hill, and I am sure they were missing some chickens. I told Sergeant Ryan to remember where those chicken coops were located, in case we got hungry.

We continued on till we approached our destination, the top of a long, sloping hill with rock outcroppings. As the sky was getting lighter, the gunny told us to find shelter under the rock ledges and get ready for a long day. It was starting to rain a little, and the wind was starting to blow into our faces. We broke out our ponchos, hunkered down under the rocks, and opened our ration packs, which filled us well whether they were tasty or not. Because it was raining, dark, and cloudy, one or two of us might be able to sneak out to get a look at that ammunition dump on the other side of the hill.

Lieutenant Skinner was in a lot of pain, and his foot was somewhat swollen, but not as badly as I'd expected. I took off his boot and sock and rubbed Bactine salve on his ankle and foot. Then I wet a bandage with cold rainwater and wrapped his ankle. We continued pouring cold water on his elevated, bandaged foot during the day, and the swelling almost disappeared. Of course, it would swell up again when he started walking, but this was a good start. It ached from the cold, but we would warm it up later. We at least tried to keep his toes dry and warm in the interim.

I changed the dressing on Corporal Park's forearm; he was still trying to keep everyone from knowing about his wound. Lieutenant Skinner told him it was good for a Purple Heart and he would buy him a steak and a beer when we got back to Japan. Park said he already had a Purple Heart and did not want any more. As a matter of fact, this was his fourth one. It turned out that I was the only one there who did not have a Purple Heart, which suited me. Things do have a way of changing.

How did I get in on this mission? Two months prior, onboard the USS *Gen. A. E. Anderson*, TAP 111, a troop transport out of Fort Mason, San Francisco, California, I was holding sick call for a bunch of marines in the ship's hospital emergency room, and that's when I met First Lieutenant Matthew Skinner, USMC. He had four or five marines who had various cuts and bruises common to jarheads not familiar with low beams, narrow hatches, and heavy steel hatch covers and doors. The lieutenant came into the treatment room after I had patched up the injuries his men had come in with, three of whom required sutures. "Hey, Doc. How much combat experience do you have?"

I replied "None, except the emergency rooms at Parris Island marine Depot, Camp LeJeune Naval Hospital and the rifle range and tank battalion at Camp LeJeune. North Carolina."

He said that sounded good enough to him and asked if I would object to him requesting me for temporary duty (TDY) with his unit in Korea. He said the corpsman assigned to his team had an accident the day before they left San Francisco, and the powers-that-be "had not found a volunteer replacement." Now tell me, what idiot would not recognize that red flag, *volunteer replacement*, to mean turn around and run away from this guy?

The good lieutenant told me to think about it and said he would talk to me again before we got to Japan. Before we got to Japan, Chief Hospital Corpsman Roy Beagle came to me and said I was going TDY to Japan for about three or four weeks. The *Anderson* was due back in Japan in five weeks, and I would rejoin the ship then.

Well, to make this long story short, I guess I volunteered for this mission. I found out the morning we were to get on the helicopter exactly where I was going and why they wanted me to accompany them. They told me I was going to accompany the marine Recon Team as "Medical Support."

They checked me out at the rifle range on the M1911A1, a .45 caliber semiautomatic pistol; the M-1 Garand .30-06 rifle; the M-1 and M-3 carbines, and the M1889 Series US Navy .38 caliber revolver. I think I surprised them all with my marksmanship and ability to handle different weapons. They issued me the .45 cal. 1911 pistol with hip holster and a .38 cal. revolver in a shoulder holster, and I chose the carbine over the Garand if I had to carry a rifle. Although I was the medical support member of the team, I was considered to be a rifleman as well. They also checked me out on an M1903A1 sniper rifle with an 8-power Unertl telescopic sight, which was carried by Sergeant Ryan. Corporal Sawkowski carried the Browning Automatic Rifle (BAR), which I had the opportunity to fire at a later date as well. The other marines were issued .45 cal. 1911 pistols and M-1 Garands. Lieutenant Skinner carried a .38 cal. revolver and a .45 cal. pistol. The South Korean soldiers had .45 cal. pistols and M-1 carbines. Everyone was issued hand grenades except me. I didn't have room for them, because of the medical packs I was carrying. We needed pack horses. But we didn't have them either.

Back to the top of the hill in North Korea, the wind was still blowing. The sun had come out around 1600 hours and disappeared over the horizon after 1730; it started getting dark and started raining again. Gunny said that was good because it gave us more cover. We had gotten a look over the hill a couple times during the day. There was our first target opportunity: a large ammunition warehouse and vehicle storage facility in the wide valley. There didn't appear to be much security. There were two small barracks on the other side of the compound, and a few soldiers milling around a building that appeared to be the mess hall. There were no guard towers except for an unmanned shed on top of the warehouse that appeared to serve that purpose.

Gunnery Sergeant Potter chose Sergeant Ryan (the demolition expert), Private Dawson, Private Mattingly, and Sergeant Kwan to accompany him down the hill to scout out the compound. They were to map out specific locations of armaments and personnel but not to make contact if at all possible. We would go back later in the night and implement the demolition operation as appropriate. The recon squad left our location at 2005, and the rest of us spread out at specific vantage points to observe their movements and be prepared to back them up if need be. Sergeant Ryan had left his sniper rifle with me, and he took my carbine. I had the advantage of the scope on his rifle, so I could see what was going on.

After about twenty minutes, we could see the shadowy figures of our men skirting the compound. They were going to check out the location of the guards and other personnel first. For over an hour, we caught glimpses of them as they moved around. Then all of a sudden, I spotted two figures moving across the compound into the warehouse. I took the scope to Lieutenant Skinner and told him what I saw.

"I told Ryan and Kwan to get as close as they could to the ammo dump but not to be too aggressive, but Ryan knows his business," he stated. After what seemed an eternity, they emerged cautiously from the building and crossed the compound. We lost sight of everyone for about twenty or thirty minutes. Then, about halfway up the hill, we saw two flashes of light. That was the signal that they would soon be arriving at our cold, wet, sloppy campsite.

The five men soon emerged from the dark underbrush carrying two cloth bags, which they set down in front of us before they flopped to the ground. Sergeant Ryan opened the bags and pulled out six boxes of Lance cheese crackers, several sticks of pepperoni, and five bottles of wine. The lieutenant turned to Gunny and asked, "Well Gunny, did you get any dope on the ammo dump or was this just a booze run?"

To which he replied, "This is going to be a turkey shoot, sir. There are not more than twenty men down there, and there are fifteen barrels of gasoline just outside the door and probably forty more inside the warehouse. We set explosives in two places in the warehouse that will set off the gas barrels and a stack of mortar shells when we strike. Kwan opened one gas barrel inside and turned it over as well as one on the outside. All we have to do is light up the gasoline on the outside, and we're in business." It sounded like a plan to me!

It was 2315 hours. They decided to set off the explosives at midnight, giving us time to eat, and then afterwards, five or six hours to move toward our next target opportunity before daylight. The Lance crackers and pepperoni were like a feast, and Lieutenant Skinner told us all that half a canteen cup of wine would help warm our bodies just fine as well as wash down the crackers. "Doc, find room for those last two bottles of wine in your gear," he added, to everyone's delight.

"Okay, you rum heads, load up and spread out. It's midnight, and they're probably all asleep down there by now. Ryan and Kwan will lead out down the middle and you four head to the left and the rest of us will take the right flank at twenty-foot intervals" said the lieutenant quietly as he pointed the directions for each of us. "Stay alert and stay safe. You can each say your own prayers as we proceed."

Thanks, I thought, but I had already started mine long ago. *This is going to be exciting*, I mused, along with, *No ... this is going to be scary, loud, and dangerous*, all at the same time.

We approached the bottom of the hill and gathered in the shadows of the underbrush and trees. Gunny laid out the plan for himself: Ryan and Kwan to enter the compound and set the final charges that would ignite the gasoline and set off the explosion inside the warehouse. The three men set off, and when they finally came out, they told us they had set twenty-minute fuses on each charge; it was time for us to move up the valley away from the exploding munitions. We headed west, and when we had traveled a couple hundred yards, Sergeant Ryan said, "Let's stop right here for a couple minutes and make sure the fireworks start on time." It wasn't long until there were two bright flashes and then the explosions, which were loud and clear and were followed by two or three tremendous blasts that shook the ground.

"I don't know what that was, but it's time for us to get the hell out of here!" shouted Gunny Sergeant Potter.

"Just like Christmas, there's a surprise in every package!" retorted Corporal Johnson.

We saw no sign of life in or around the compound.

About a half hour later, we came across a small encampment, but there were no soldiers to be seen. Two trucks sat parked beside the tents. "They're up on that hill looking at the explosion," said Private Finch.

"Get in that truck in front and disable the other one, and we'll put some distance between us before they know what's going on," ordered Lieutenant Skinner. "Grab those weapons over there so they can't start shooting when they discover what we're up to."

Corporal Park got into the driver's seat and started the engine on the first try as the rest of us piled into the bed of the truck. Sawkowski yanked the coil wire from the other vehicle and we sped off just as he jumped in. We heard the shouts from the surprised North Korean soldiers and a couple pistol shots rang out, but no one was hit. Sergeant Kwan said we would be able to drive about ten miles before we came to any civilization.

The truck bucked and bounced over the bumpy road, but it still beat walking through the wet, mountainous terrain in the dark. "There are headlights up ahead!" shouted Park. "It looks like a jeep." He slowed down as we approached the jeep, and just as we got beside it, Park swerved into it, knocking it off the road. There were four soldiers seated in it, and a couple of our men fired at the enemy as we sped off.

"It's time to get outta this truck and get back on the trail, before we run into something we can't handle!" said Lieutenant Skinner.

"Aw, come on, Lieutenant. There ain't nothing a few marines can't handle," said Mattingly, "besides, I could get used to riding everywhere we go." At that point, the lieutenant told Park to find an opening in the trees and look for a place to hide the truck. He soon pulled over and drove about fifty yards back through the wooded area. We reluctantly unloaded.

Sergeant Ryan had us pile the confiscated Chinese and Russian rifles and ammunition in the cab of the truck. He got in the truck on the passenger side, placed a hand grenade under the gas pedal, and attached a wire from the pin of the grenade to the handle of the driver's door. He slowly got out of the passenger side of the vehicle and locked the door. "Whoever opens that door will get the biggest and last surprise of his life," exclaimed Ryan. It was time for us to move on.

We walked on for miles and were about halfway up yet another hill. There was no way to go around these, because it was just one hill after another in every direction. Corporal Park spotted an outcropping of rocks and thought it would be a good place to rest for a while. As we slid up under the rock ledges, Lieutenant Skinner suggested this would be a good spot to spend the day, since the sky was already starting to show signs of daylight.

"Doc, see if anyone needs a little bit of wine to warm those bones again. Not as much this time; we might want it to last a day or two," said Lieutenant Skinner.

It was now 0615, and we could hear Korean voices coming from a distance. It sounded like it was probably a military encampment, so Gunny sent Kwan and Park to check it out. He then asked Private Dawson to take the first watch and for the rest of us to get some rest and try to sleep if we could. Gunny always seemed to be awake and on watch, but he sat down this time and sipped a little wine. The injured lieutenant was already asleep. The wine and the morphine shot I gave him had knocked him out.

Sergeant Kwan and Corporal Park had been gone over two hours, and Sergeant Ryan was getting ready to go looking for them when they showed up. "There are over a thousand soldiers in that encampment over that next hill. They have two Russian helicopters, large trucks, weapon carriers, jeeps, artillery, and at least two Russian tanks. They're loading troops into at least six of the trucks, and two weapons carriers are pulling artillery pieces," Sergeant Kwan reported to the gunny and the lieutenant, who was now awake.

"They're probably heading back to the ammunition depot that we took care of last night. Let's sit tight until they move out, and we will go take another look," said Skinner.

Sergeant Kwan replied, "That camp is not on our map or photos, so it has been there less than four weeks. There may be others we don't know about up the road."

Corporal Park said, "They had a Russian flag in addition to their North Korean flag flying at the front gate. I've never seen that before."

What have we gotten ourselves into now? I thought.

"Everybody settle down and stay outta sight for the rest of the day, gyrenes," said Gunnery Sergeant Potter using the mixed nickname for GIs and marines. "We will need to be rested tonight. Doc, you and Corporal Johnson take the next watch. Sergeant Ryan and Private Smith will spell ya' in two hours. I'll let you know when it's time."

Johnson and I sat through our two-hour watch with nothing to see, but we were still hearing a lot of activity from the encampment over the next hilltop. We heard the tanks start up twice, but they must have just been checking them out and charging their batteries. I went over and shook Ryan and Smith, letting them know it was time for their watch. I looked over and Gunny was still sawing logs like crazy. That was the longest I had ever seen him sleep. It didn't take long for me to snooze off either. The next thing I knew, Sergeant Johnson was punching me awake and saying it was 1700 hours and we needed to get something to eat and get ready to move on. The Lance cheese crackers were gone, but we still had pepperoni to go with the rations. No wine this time, because we would need all our faculties for what was ahead of us tonight and tomorrow.

Kwan, Park, and Ryan came back to our little campsite from another recon trip to check out the North Korean encampment. Sergeant Ryan reported that the enemy soldiers were loading up more troops into the trucks. He said it looked like they were moving to another location, because they were loading furniture and supplies from the large tents and over half of the soldiers' tents were gone. The tanks were gone too, and it appeared they were fueling up the helicopters. The lieutenant and Gunny asked a few more questions, then decided to just make notes of all this and move on around the camp, not starting anything we might not be able to finish. The sergeant had taken two rolls of pictures and documented everything he could from the hillside.

There were several anti-aircraft gun emplacements we knew of about eight miles away, and we'd been heading for them when we found this camp. It was really a big find for us, especially after spotting the Russian flag, but it was time to move out. We cleaned up our site, buried trash that we were not taking with us, and hit the trail. It was not much of a trail, but we had to make sure we steered clear of the North Koreans and Russians. "They're going to the ammo depot to see what they can find," surmised Lieutenant Skinner.

We walked quickly over hill and dell for several hours before we could relax enough to slow down and take a breath. In spite of all the walking, we were pretty well rested after sleeping most of the day and getting a chance to put on dry socks. Lieutenant Skinner had thrown away his crutch and was getting around better than we expected. I told him it was just the outstanding medical care he had received! About 2015 we started again, but Sergeant Ryan called out, "Get back under those trees—there's a helicopter coming up the valley with his spotlights shining down! It looks like he is searching for us."

The big helicopter slowly thundered by within thirty yards of our hiding spot. Then it went out of sight, and Gunny brought us out again, just as we heard the 'copter coming back around. We moved back into the trees, and Gunny said, "Corporal Sawkowski, when he gets back into clear view, open up on his cockpit with that BAR. Private Dawson, when Ski opens up, you launch a grenade through the open door. Private Mattingly, you may as well launch another grenade at the base of the blades. That should get their attention."

My God, I thought, *If you're going to do it, do it right.*

The helicopter came around a little closer, almost overhead, and was swinging back and forth, which moved the light around on the ground. And then, BANG! BANG! BANG! Ski was tapping them off one at a time in quick succession. Sparks were flying all over the cockpit. As soon as Ski cut loose, Dawson put a grenade right through the open door with his Garand grenade launcher, and at the same time, Mattingly shot a grenade through the cowl of the 'copter motor. The wounded chopper made a couple rolling flips and hit the ground with an explosion within fifty yards of our attack.

Suddenly, another SWOOSH, SWOOSH, SWOOSH from that second big Russian helicopter was coming right at us. Evidently, he saw the explosion and was coming back to check it out. He was climbing higher up, but was still in range. Lieutenant Skinner yelled, "Everybody cut loose on him! Sawkowski, open up automatic with that BAR! Hit him with those grenade launchers! Everybody else, hit that communist son-of-a-bitch with everything you've got—*NOW, NOW!*"

I've never heard such a commotion in my life. Those guys did not know what hit them as the helicopter nosed into the ground within fifty yards of the first one, making an explosion just as big.

The next thing I heard was, "Corpsman, Corpsman! We've got two men down!" I looked around and someone was lying face down. Private Smith was sitting on the ground holding his left shoulder, blood everywhere. I ran to Smith and got a tourniquet on his shoulder and had Finch hold it tightly. I went over and found Corporal Johnson face down as Sergeant Ryan was turning him over slowly. There was blood all over his face and more blood on his left side. But after checking him, it looked like a bullet had grazed his scalp and another bullet had probably fractured a rib, but it seemed to have glanced off also.

I asked Sergeant Ryan to clean Johnson's wounds and bandage them, while I turned my attention to Private Smith. I leaned him back against Finch and cut his uniform from around the wound. It was a clean shot through his shoulder as big as my thumb and took bone from his shoulder socket with it. I gave him a shot of morphine and started cleaning out the wound; then I packed it to control bleeding. I bandaged it tightly, wrapped it, and then bound his arm across his stomach.

"Hey, where's Dawson?" Someone shouted. "I've not seen Dawson!"

We all looked around, and I heard Lieutenant Skinner, "Over here, Doc, come quick."

There was Dawson flat on his back with his Garand grenade launcher still attached, pointed up into the night sky. I could see from the light of the crashes, and when a couple flashlights came in, there were three large dark spots in a row across his chest. *Semper Fi, Private Dawson!*

"There must have been a machine gun firing from the doorway of the helicopter," I said. "I thought I saw flashes coming out the door when I was shooting at them. That's what hit all three of them." From the looks of Smitty's shoulder and Dawson's chest, they were firing a .50 caliber machine gun at us. There was nothing left of the 'copters to check that out, but it didn't matter now.

"Gunny, let's pull everyone back into the trees and find a burial space for Private Dawson, no, make that *Corporal* Dawson; he was promoted to corporal this morning," said a visibly shaken Lieutenant Skinner. "He'll have a Christian burial, and then we've got to get out of here. Sergeant Ryan, mark this location on two maps. I'll carry one, and give one to Doc."

After a solemn forty-five minutes, we had dug a grave. Each one of us, including Private Smith and Corporal Johnson, removed some dirt from the grave for our brother. Lieutenant Skinner honored Corporal Dawson with honest, Christian words of praise for the fallen marine and a moving prayer followed by the Lord's Prayer, which was shared by all of us.

We fashioned a stretcher for Private Smith out of tree limbs and ponchos, since he was too weak to walk. I gave him another shot of morphine and made him as comfortable as possible. I then checked on Corporal Johnson and decided to tape his ribs before he started walking. He refused the morphine for now. After everyone was taken care of and we all got a good drink of water, we started the trek on up the mountains. The map designated them as hills, but those were mountains.

We could hear engine sounds in the distance, and it sounded like trucks instead of helicopters or airplanes. We felt it best to keep on walking at this time and to keep a sharp lookout for any other signs of trouble that might arise. I'd had enough excitement for the rest of the week. It was now 2240, and we still had a long way to go before daylight, with the stretcher and walking-wounded marines. Johnson was gasping for breath already but hadn't complained one word.

Around 0100 hours, the lieutenant called for a rest stop. Smitty was asleep on the stretcher, which scared me, but he was okay. The morphine was working. I asked Johnson how he was doing, but he just flopped back on the ground and closed his eyes. I knew him well enough not to ask any more questions until he started talking himself. He would speak up when he needed something. I checked on the others, reminding them all to put on some dry socks while we were stopped and use a little foot powder, too. I sat down with the gunnery sergeant after Lieutenant Skinner walked away into the tree line by himself, which I knew we shouldn't do. Gunny said to just leave him alone for now.

Lieutenant Skinner enlisted in the marines as a private near the end of World War II when he was eighteen years old. He served four years before he got out and attended the University of Iowa for four years. He enrolled in their ROTC program and graduated with a degree in business and re-entered the Marine Corps as a second lieutenant. Within six months, he was shipped to Korea and was soon promoted to first lieutenant. The gunnery sergeant had served with him when the lieutenant was a private and Gunny was a corporal. They were good friends as well as outstanding professionals working together.

At 0145, Lieutenant Skinner asked Sergeant Kwan where our location was on the map and how much farther we had to travel till we reached the next objective.

"We're approximately six miles out," answered Kwan, "and at the rate we are traveling and the terrain we must cross, I doubt we'll make it before daylight unless we split up and the demolition team moves ahead."

"No," retorted the lieutenant and the gunnery sergeant simultaneously.

"We will not split up," said Skinner.

"We arrived together and we travel together," added Gunny.

The lieutenant turned to me and said, "Doc, we'll move out as soon as you say we can. I can help with the stretcher." I told him to take care of his ankle and we would carry Smitty. "We've got everyone ready, sir, and we better get moving," I replied.

We moved around the side of the mountain as the moon came out, making it almost bright as day. This was the first time we had seen the moon that bright since we arrived. We had begun to move at angles on the hillsides and to move from one to another instead of going straight up and down. It was a little faster and a whole lot more comfortable to travel that way. It was really scary to be out in the open with the moon that bright, but we could definitely see where we were going. We could see a wide valley ahead of us, before we reached the next mountain. There was a large group of trees ahead and possibly a small river or stream. Probably no surprises from here on.

After we reached the rim of the valley, Gunny sent Kwan and Park ahead to scout the trees. Something just didn't feel right about this valley. They left me with Johnson and Smith and spread out to cover our flanks. After forty minutes, Kwan and Park came back and reported there was no evidence of the enemy, nor any sign they had been there recently. Lieutenant Skinner moved us out quietly but kept us spread apart as much as possible. I was carrying the front of the stretcher and Finch was at the back. Johnson was walking beside us with his Garand at ready. In spite of how we felt, we made it to the tree line and on to a small mountain stream.

As we approached the stream, we could see the outlines of a small bridge across the water. "There ain't no way in hell I'm going across that bridge," stated Sergeant Ryan. "We all know that bridge is booby-trapped." I think everyone agreed with him.

Park suggested that he move upstream and Kwan downstream to find a narrow, shallow place to cross. Within ten minutes, Park found a spot, and as soon as Kwan returned, we moved upstream and were across the six to eight inches of water in another ten minutes. We looked ahead to a line of trees between us and the next hill as the moon was starting to go behind some clouds. Kwan and Park led us through the trees, and as the ground started to rise toward the mountain, I heard a little noise to my right.

There was a North Korean soldier trotting out of the wooded area. He was just as surprised to see us as we were to see him. I swung my carbine around and started firing from about thirty feet away before he was able to get his rifle from his shoulder. I kept pulling the trigger until he hit the ground.

Corporal Johnson patted me on the shoulder, and said, "I think you got him, Doc. Do you want me to check his pulse?"

To which Gunny added, "I'm glad he didn't have a 500-round drum on that thing or we would have been here all night."

I didn't know what to say, so I went over and checked him out myself. He was lying on his back on top of his rifle, dead for sure, and then I noticed something halfway out of his jacket. When I bent over, I could see his face. He didn't look to be sixteen years of age. There was a packet of pictures in his jacket, and all I could see was the face of a young woman holding a baby. I didn't look at any other pictures; I just stuck them back into his jacket pocket. Finch and Park pulled his body back into the trees, disposed of his rifle, and we moved on. We didn't hear any more footsteps or any other sounds. The young soldier must have been by himself returning to his camp. Kwan said it was not unusual for a local soldier to visit his home occasionally at night and return to camp before dawn.

Speaking of dawn, it was already beginning to get light, with the moon barely peaking through the clouds from time to time. "We just need to get up this next hill," said Kwan, "and we will be able to see our objective," That hill took us nearly two hours to climb, and it was daylight when we finished. It took all our strength, but everyone wanted to see what the other side of the hill held for us. Kwan, Park, and Gunny moved on around to check out the next valley. They came back and said we were in the right place. They could see six anti-aircraft gun emplacements from their vantage point.

We rested awhile, and I took care of the medical needs of Smitty and Johnson. Private Smith sat up off the stretcher for a while. He was weak and dizzy, but he didn't want to miss anything. I cleaned, medicated, and dressed his wound, which looked surprisingly good. There wasn't as much damage as I first thought, but he still needed surgery. Corporal Johnson was doing well but had some very sore ribs. Lieutenant Skinner's ankle had swollen again, and I told him he needed to stay off it and elevate it for the next eight to ten hours.

I went around to take a look at the valley. "Where are the guns? I asked Kwan. "All I can see are several stacks of wood.".

"Those stacks of wood are hollow boxes, designed to look like stacked lumber and swivel around as covers to the gun emplacements. They move the lumber back and raise the guns. They are very effective anti-aircraft weapons. Now let's get some rest and we'll take care of them tonight."

Sleep came easily that day for all of us. We had a good hiding place in the underbrush. The clouds soon moved out, and the sun shown down on us, warming our bodies and souls. I closed my eyes and slept until I was awakened by Ski for my watch, from noon until 1500 hours. I got a bite to eat as we kept watch and remembered that I had not eaten anything before I went to sleep earlier that morning. Your appetite is not as good as during normal times, but every little bite tastes great.

By the time my watch was over, I was sleepy again. I lay down and closed my eyes, but all I could see was that young woman and her baby—the image wouldn't go away. I couldn't sleep and got up, relieving Corporal Johnson early from his watch duties, so he could get some sleep.

Close to dusk, everyone got up and started moving around. Private Smith insisted that he did not need the stretcher anymore. Johnson was his usual ornery self, and the lieutenant was walking around, so we were in pretty good shape. Kwan, Park, Ryan, and Finch went down into the valley for recon, and Ryan would set charges on all six guns if he could. I gave Ryan my carbine, and he handed me his 03 scoped sniper rifle. Then in a blink, they were out of sight. There was heavy underbrush all the way down the hill, which would keep them concealed from the enemy. It would also conceal the enemy from us if they were there.

After forty minutes, we could see our guys' shadowy figures move across the valley from one location to the next. It took them over an hour to make it back to the bottom of the mountain. It was another hour before the group made it back to our campsite. "We got 'em all set," Ryan said. "We found eight guns instead of six; two of the guns just had flat covers over them. They are all tied together to go off at the same time. All we have to do is fire 'em up. We didn't find a single defender and it doesn't look like there has been anyone around since that last good rain. Everyone must have gone over to the ammo dump. I don't know why, there's nothing there but a hole in the ground."

"Gather around, Gyrenes," said Lieutenant Skinner. "Doc, check Private Smith and see if he can walk with us or if he needs the stretcher. See if Corporal Johnson needs anything, and before you ask, my ankle is good. I may have to walk with a stick, but I'll get there. Then we go down to the clearing to get into position for Sergeant Ryan to set off those explosives, and then we'll head southwest toward the DMZ."

Smitty was running a fever and seemed too weak to be walking. I got him back onto the stretcher, gave him a shot of penicillin, and had privates Mattingly and Finch carry him. Johnson said, "I'm fine, let's go." That's all it took for me, and I reported back to the lieutenant that we were all set. He had the others ready to go do what they already knew how to do.

"Let's go blow up something!" said Gunny.

Moving down the hill in the thick underbrush and trees in the dark, moonless night was slow-going. There were no sounds or sightings of the North Korean soldiers at the anti-aircraft defense station. With no buildings visible, you can be assured that there's a well-stocked cave hidden in the nearby vicinity. Sergeants Ryan and Kwan moved down the hill ahead of us with Corporal Sawkowski and his BAR behind them as backup. The rest of us veered to the left to be out of the way when the explosives took out the anti-aircraft weapons and ammunition. The ammo was stored in lockers behind the guns down in covered wells. This should be another magnificent set of explosions.

We moved our men to the west side of the gun emplacements as Ryan worked his magic with the timers on the explosives. He didn't take but ten minutes to finish the connections, and the three of them came over to join the rest of us. "I set these fuses to go in about thirty minutes, so let's move out," said Ryan.

We started out and heard a vehicle coming from the east side of the valley. Since we were headed west, away from the vehicle, the lieutenant moved us into a line of trees. "Just sit here and wait," he said quietly. "This will get really interesting if they find the charges."

Sergeant Ryan replied, "They won't find them in the short time they have before they start exploding. They were set for 2135 to 2140, and it's now 2128. Just hang loose."

We could see the dimmed lights of two vehicles pulled over to the middle of the gun wells. Sergeant Ryan was looking through his sniper scope and said, "There is one truck with several guys in it and a jeep with two or three men. They are all standing around in a group."

Lieutenant Skinner motioned for us to stay down and be quiet.

I looked at my watch with a covered light and it was 2135 ... then 2136 ... and then ... *BOOM!* After that, there were several more explosions that shook the valley, and then the ammunition started shooting out of the gun wells up into the air. It was quite a sight.

"Okay, children, let's move out of here. I don't think any of them got out of those explosions, but follow me away from this valley before anymore eyes in the sky come looking for us," said Lieutenant Skinner rather loudly. "We will have to keep moving all night to the west of this next hill and then head south. We are about thirty miles north of the DMZ and hot showers, hot food, and a surgeon for Smitty."

We trudged along all night, taking turns carrying Private Smith on his stretcher and also finding another crutch for Lieutenant Skinner. His ankle was swelling again, and he was struggling to walk. About 0200, Gunny called us to a halt for a longer rest stop beside a small stream with a secure area for me to use a flashlight and check all the wounds. Smitty had started to groan along the way, bounced by the stretcher as we walked, and he was still running a fever. I increased the penicillin dosage, removed the dressing, removed more debris, sprinkled Sulfa powder into the wound, repacked, and bandaged the wound in his shoulder. We really needed to get him back to a hospital for surgery, because I had done all I could do out here.

I called Corporal Johnson over and made him sit down so I could examine his wounds. He didn't want to but he did. I took the bandage off his head, cleaned the area, sprinkled the Sulfa powder into the wound, and rebandaged it. I wanted to suture the gash closed, but the bullet left a groove over a half inch wide, and the sutures just wouldn't close it. I left that for the surgeons to take care of. He definitely had a broken rib that I had taped, and I just left it alone.

Lieutenant Skinner was sprawled out under a tree with his foot elevated on a backpack and appeared to be asleep. I walked over and he didn't move, so I just left him alone. I made the rounds talking with everyone, passed out a few APC (Aspirin, Phenactin and Caffeine) tablets for aches and pains, and they all seemed to be doing well considering what we had been through. Gunny told everyone to get some rest and he would keep the watch. "We'll start out again about 0415, unless something changes. You all need the rest."

Gunny started waking us all a little after 0400, and it was hard to get those eyelids open. "I started to fire a couple rounds into the air, but I figured half of you would probably shoot back," he said, kiddingly. "Doc, make sure all these Gyrenes are shipshape and ready to go. We've wasted too much time already." I knew he'd given us the extra rest so Lieutenant Skinner and Private Smith would be able to travel.

We were all stiff and sore, but we were also eager to get back below the DMZ for some hot food and some restful sleep. Those thoughts made the travel more palatable as we stepped them off. We were walking south on a valley trail that had been used frequently from all appearances. Sergeant Kwan said this was the main path from Sapo, North Korea, to Chorwan, South Korea, for the locals.

"Lieutenant, my father's oldest brother lives just two miles from here, and we had better stop near there for the day. Maybe my uncle can find us a ride down within sight of the border."

"Sounds great, Sarge. You know we appreciate that offer. I think I saw everyone step out a little faster when you said that," mused Lieutenant Skinner. That did make the walk a little easier.

Before long, Sergeant Kwan told us it would be a good time for us to stop here and pull back into the shadow of the trees. "I'll go ahead and talk to my uncle and check out the area. Corporal Park will shadow me, since I am not going to carry a weapon. It will be safer that way." They walked on ahead, and Corporal Johnson followed behind Park just to be sure.

It was thirty minutes before Kwan and his Uncle Huang Pak slowly walked back our way. The sergeant made introductions all around to his cautious uncle. Remember, we were still in North Korea, and he would have to live here after we leave. This turned out to be routine for Mr. Pak. He had probably rescued hundreds of American, South Korean, and other allied soldiers and funneled them back to the South with the help of several of his neighbors. He had Kwan tell us to relax for a couple hours, while he arranged our transportation out of there.

Private Smith tapped me on the leg when I walked by his stretcher and told me, "When we leave here, I'm walking with the rest of you. You guys have carried me far enough, and I will do my part from here on."

"Smitty, you have more than done your part, but we will leave the stretcher here. I will take it apart and put the ponchos in our gear. We don't want to leave any evidence that we have been here," I replied.

Corporal Johnson and Lieutenant Skinner both checked out fairly well, so we would all sit back and wait for our ride to the border.

It was 1015 hours before Mr. Pak came back for us. We had heard the engines of two or three vehicles and really didn't know what to expect. It turned out that he and two of his farmer neighbors had to take loads of produce to the market and would conceal us with the vegetables. He said we would not be traveling any of the main roads, so we should not encounter any of the North Korean soldiers. The military all but demanded the civilians use the back roads and leave the main roads to the army and police.

It was 1100 by the time we were split up and situated in the trucks amid all the best smelling vegetables you could imagine. The lieutenant objected to us being separated like that, but he was convinced that it would be the safest and the only way they could transport us. I was riding in the same truck as Smith, Johnson, and Finch. After we started rolling, I looked over to my left, and there were dozens of bunches of turnips and turnip greens. Anyone that knows me can certainly imagine what happened next. I reached over and grabbed a bunch and bit into the largest, sweetest, juiciest turnip that I have ever enjoyed in my life. I ate two of them and my stomach was already aching, so I stuck the bunch back down into the basket.

We moved on through three small villages without incident. The trucks did not have to stop as we moved through the countryside and small towns. Mr. Pak advised us to keep out of sight and not take any chances of being seen and reported. He didn't say anything about not eating turnips! Just before noon, the trucks pulled over. I heard Kwan say to Skinner, "My uncle says they can drive around through the back trails and carry us across the Demilitarized Zone into South Korea. They often take that route when they sell produce in Chorwan."

The lieutenant replied, "That's the best news we've had in over a week, Sergeant. Let's get 'em rolling!"

I don't know about everyone else, but I think I held my breath for the next half hour. When the trucks stopped, the laughter started in the first truck and rolled on back like dominos to us. We were back on friendly soil thanks to the five brave Koreans!

"Thank you, Mr. Pak!" we all exclaimed. "We are grateful to you and your neighbors for your friendship as well as your assistance."

"God Bless you, sir," said Lieutenant Skinner as he shook hands with Mr. Pak and gave him a big bear hug. The Korean men all laughed as they backed away, bowing, and they got into their trucks to go sell their produce at the open market—minus two turnips. You won't believe what a stomachache I had!

A South Korean army officer came out of the building where we were dropped off. He rushed us all inside and showed us into a small meeting room. "We need to get an ambulance for Smitty," I said to Gunny.

"Right you are, Doc," he replied. "Lieutenant, Doc wants us to get

Private Smith to a hospital before we do anything. He needs surgery now."

He acknowledged and went back out into the front office and came right back. "They have an ambulance here, and there is a hospital with American Army doctors less than thirty minutes away."

"Do you want me to go with him to the hospital?" I asked, wanting to make sure they knew what I had done for Smitty. "Negative, Doc. We only have permission for Smith to leave at this time."

Wow, what do you mean permission to leave, I thought to myself but only replied "Yes, *sir!*" We took Smitty to the ambulance where the driver and two Korean army medics were waiting. Each of us wished him luck and said our good-byes. I never found out how he made out after he was flown to Japan the next day.

We stayed sprawled out in the meeting room for over an hour. Thank goodness, there were two rest rooms adjacent to the room where we could relieve ourselves in comfort and finally wash our face and hands. Then the door opened; a US Marine colonel came in and asked if anyone was hungry. "Come on out the back door. Across the alley is a mess hall with a secure area where you men can eat together." It was afternoon, but those scrambled eggs, pancakes, sausage, bacon, buttered toast, grits, fried potatoes, fried apples, and fruit cocktail were a feast. And we had HOT COFFEE, as well as orange juice and milk.

Between bites, Lieutenant Skinner said, "Listen to me a minute while we eat, before anyone else comes in. The colonel is waiting for us to finish eating, and we can stay out here as long as need be. Do not speak to anyone on this base without permission, for anything. When we go back in there, the colonel will start our debriefing session. He will talk to us as a group and that won't last but about thirty or forty minutes. He's been there, so he knows how we are feeling. Don't ask questions and answer only what he asks you, nothing more. When he has completed his preliminary session, we will all be escorted to a segregated barracks area where hot showers, clean clothing, and clean beds are waiting."

We probably ate for forty-five minutes, and everyone grabbed another cup of coffee to take back to the debriefing session. Back in the meeting room, we all found a seat around the table, and the colonel entered. "Attention on deck!" shouted Gunny as we all popped up.

"At ease, men," countered the colonel. "I am Colonel Watkins. You men think you have been into North Korea. *That didn't happen!* You men think you were in combat with a hostile enemy. *That didn't happen!* You think you suffered injuries and lost a brother. *That didn't happen!* Now listen to me. No one outside this room will hear from you about where you have been or what has happened. You will not tell any other member of your service a word of this. You will not tell your wife or your girlfriend and, hell, you will not even tell your Mama and Daddy. Now, tomorrow at 0700, you will muster in the front hall of your barracks. You will be debriefed separately and will muster at the mess hall at 1300 hours tomorrow. We will have one more meal together, and you'll be sent back to your respective duty stations immediately. I won't take anymore of your time, because some of you may be tired. You have done one helluva'n outstanding job and I salute your dedication to the Corps. Now, Doc, do any of these men, or you, need any medical attention before we leave for the barracks?"

"No sir, Colonel, I've already talked to each man. We're ready for a good night's sleep."

"Thanks Doc, good job. By the way, I hear by the way of the grapevine that none of you want the doc to take his carbine to the barracks, right?"

Every one let out a big laugh, and I turned bright red. "No one better comment," I replied to the room full of tired, dirty, but happy warriors of the best kind.

The showers were hot, and you could hardly see across the shower room stalls for the steam. Within an hour, every man was showered, shaved, and ready for bed. It was just getting dark, but we were about ready to sack out. Just then, Colonel Watkins came through the door followed by two marines carrying a large cooler, and the colonel sat a box on the table beside the cooler.

The colonel dismissed the marines and turned to us. "I thought you might want a hamburger and a beer if you got hungry during the night."

Thanks were expressed by everyone, and I said, "Excuse me, sir. We brought something back for you." I went over to my bunk and pulled a large bottle of wine out of my backpack and handed it to the colonel. "We had one left over," I said.

He laughed and said, "You damned corpsmen don't miss a thing, do you. Keep up the good work." Then he shook my hand, saluted us all, and left. We all opened a beer but not many finished even one, and we were in bed asleep.

Reveille came early for us, at 0600 hours. We got up and got dressed. Then the lieutenant and Gunny escorted us to the mess hall. I was surprised that they stayed in the same barracks with us, but we were in isolation, for sure. We went through the mess line as a group and were asked how we wanted our eggs and had a choice of bacon, sausage, and ham. Then there were choices of fruits, juices, milk, coffee, pancakes, biscuits, and toast. Don't tell anyone, but half these guys had eaten cold hamburgers and beer before we came over for breakfast, but that didn't slow them down when we got into the chow line.

We finished eating all we could and were taken back to the same meeting room. Colonel Watkins was waiting for us with a stack of papers. I recognized them immediately as our individual orders. "Come on in, gentlemen. There are doughnuts and coffee on the table in the back in case there wasn't enough grub for you in the mess hall." Believe it or not, a line formed at the food table.

"Lieutenant Skinner, you have an outstanding team here that you have put together. You and your men are commended for what you have accomplished in a few short days."

"They weren't so damned short," Gunny replied. Everyone laughed, including the colonel.

"Poor choice of words on my part, Gunny. We all know how long those days can be. Now, there has been a slight change of plans for your final debriefing. Go back to the barracks where a detail is waiting for you to turn in all your gear. You came in with nothing, and you will leave the same way—no souvenirs! After that, a bus will be waiting to take you to the airport to fly you to Tachikawa Air Base where you will be separated for your final debriefing." A cheer went up immediately, but we knew to keep it short. "I will be there to keep you guys under control and, by the way, thanks for the wine. My wife asked where we could get some more, but I told her it was not likely."

Sergeant Ryan stood up and said, "In all due respect, sir. Don't thank us, thank the doc." After another hearty laugh, he added. "Just kidding, sir."

"One more thing before we go. Let's bow our heads for a couple minutes' prayer for Corporal Dawson, our missing brother. We all wish he was here with us today." After about two minutes, the colonel led us in the Lord's Prayer.

After we turned in our weapons and gear, we were informed that all items were accounted for and the bus was waiting. We went out to the parking compound carrying our "ditty bags" with our toilet articles that were issued here; nothing else was to go. Nothing else except for the case of beer that magically appeared in the back of the bus. We settled in and got underway and were all surprised that the colonel was riding with us. "Okay Gunny, I don't know where you hid it, but break out the beer." I couldn't believe it—as strict and as by-the-book the colonel, lieutenant, and gunnery sergeant were—but the colonel got the first beer.

We then found out that those three, plus Sergeant Ryan, had a history going back over ten years. The colonel made sure they stayed in close contact when anything was planned that required their respective talents. They all knew what the other was thinking and going to do. As we arrived at the airport a couple hours later, and after two bathroom breaks, the colonel said, "All right, shape up, you gyrenes. Put all the trash in the back of the bus, and the driver will clean up after you—*this time*." Look sharp boarding the plane. There will be a couple other people on the plane that you don't know, and you will keep it that way. Don't talk to anyone."

The bus pulled up to the gate and the MP waved us through when the colonel stood up beside the driver. We then drove out on to the tarmac, and there sat a Japanese airliner. The colonel led us off the bus onto the airliner, and there were four high-ranking marine officers in the front seats. They didn't look at us, and we didn't look at them. The colonel didn't have to worry about us talking to them, that's for sure. We got seats as far back as we could, buckled up, and the door slammed shut. The engines coughed to life, warmed up for about five minutes, and we pulled out onto the runway and took off without stopping. As the plane reached the cruising altitude, the smoking light came on, and we unbuckled.

Everyone was then surprised to see the two-star marine general stand up and come back toward us carrying two cartons of Camel cigarettes. "You can't smoke 'em if you don't got 'em. Great job, men," he said with a smile and salute; then he turned around and went back to his seat.

That was a quiet trip to Japan. We all slept most of the way, and very few words were heard. After we landed at Tachikawa and taxied to the tarmac, an Air Force Chevrolet Suburban and a bus pulled up to the plane. We waited while the marine brass got into the Suburban, and then we got out of our seats and went to the bus for a ride to one of the Air Force buildings on base. This was the quietest this group had ever been. The food and sleep had calmed everyone, and it was as if we all had jet lag.

Now the fun began. We were ushered into a large conference room with a long, walnut, glass-top table and lush, upholstered chairs. The carpet was almost as deep as grass. "I would as soon lie down on the carpet as sit in the chairs," quipped Private Finch. That's one of the few words we ever heard out of the quiet, Ohio farm boy.

"Have a seat, men. I am General Billings." It was the two-star general from the airplane. "Congratulations on a job well done. We are all proud of you and the commandant is aware of your accomplishments. All of you have Top Secret Clearance, so you know how vital it is to our country's security that you maintain your silence. It's as if none of the events of the past ten days ever happened. I know you have heard this before, and you will hear it again more times than you like. So be it." He turned to another marine officer behind him who had only one star. "Do you have anything to add, General Starky?"

"No, I think you covered it all, but I do want to add my gratitude to these fine marines, the fine Navy corpsman, and our friends in the South Korean army. Doc, I think your experience will be the only story told, although in another context. Lieutenant Skinner, keep him on your list." I could feel my face turn red, and everyone laughed loudly, and Sergeant Ryan slapped me on the back.

"I didn't think we were supposed to talk about this experience that didn't happen," I said to more laughter.

"Okay, back to business," the general said as the room grew quiet again, thank goodness. "The captain will take over now. Semper Fi, men," he said, with another salute. "Semper Fi, sir!"

"I am Captain Blakenship. I am your debriefing officer," he said curtly. "As I call your name, you will go with the officer assigned to you. You will ask no questions and answer only those questions asked of you. We are not your chaplains! Now, Lieutenant Skinner ..."

The captain went on down the list of names, and I was the last one before the Koreans. We were taken into private offices. "I am Second Lieutenant Smith, Doc; have a seat and relax. This will be a casual but serious meeting. Now, what was your role in this mission?"

"What mission, sir?" I asked. Lieutenant Smith smiled and said, "That hasn't started yet. You need to talk to me and answer the questions just like the general said."

"Just practicing, sir," I replied, "but as a Navy corpsman, I was the medical support for this reconnaissance team."

The questions went on for two hours or more in great detail. We only had one restroom break, and the lieutenant accompanied me to the door of the head when I took it. I ended up recalling the entire mission for this *Lieutenant Smith*, which I was sure was not his real name. No one was wearing the usual name badges.

"All right, Doc," he said, reaching across the table to shake hands, "There is a car waiting for you that will take you to the bus station for your trip to Yokohama where you will wait for your ship to dock."

I asked if we were not going to the mess hall first with lunch with the other men before we left, but he said that would not happen. "Most everyone else has already left. Lieutenant Skinner said he would see you in Yokohama. Here is twenty dollars spending money for you. I know you were not allowed to bring any with you. Have a safe trip, Doc. I enjoyed meeting you." And he shook my hand again and led me to the car. The driver opened the back door for me, and I was soon on my way to Yokohama.

At the bus station, the driver accompanied me to the bus, but we stopped by the snack bar. I ordered a cheeseburger and a Coke. The driver said, "Here you go, Doc. I will pay for that. Lieutenant Smith said you were not to pay for anything before you left."

"Thanks, Private. I should have ordered a steak," I replied.

"If you had time," he replied, "that's what you would get, but your bus leaves in ten minutes." I finished the burger and fries they had added to my tray. I had forgotten how good a small bottled Coke could taste. The driver then escorted me to the bus and wished me luck.

I climbed onto the bus and heard a familiar voice say, "Come on back and have a seat, Doc." There sat Lieutenant Skinner near the back of the dark blue Air Force bus. "You guys are going to make sure I don't go anywhere alone, aren't you?" I heard a laugh to my right and there sat Gunnery Sergeant Potter and Sergeant Ryan. "Damn, I think it's you three who can't go anywhere alone," I laughed.

"Well, it may be the four of us for a while, Corpsman. We'll talk when we get on down the road. Now, Gunny, do we have any refreshments?"

Yes, you guessed it. Here came four Budweisers. There were not but three other people on the bus, and they were up near the front. I don't think anyone would have said anything anyway.

We talked for a while about nothing in particular, and then everyone was pretty quiet for the rest of the trip to Yokohama. As we approached the Navy base, the driver asked Lieutenant Skinner which facility we were going to. The lieutenant gave him a building number, and the driver knew where it was located. The bus pulled through the gate and drove on to the Administration Building. We then checked in at the front desk and were told that a car would pick us up. Lieutenant Skinner asked about my ship and the yeoman behind the desk looked it up and said it would arrive in eight days at Pier 15. Lieutenant Skinner thanked the yeoman and told him, "Cancel the car. We're not far from where we're going, and we'll just walk."

After we left the building and walked up the street a ways, Lieutenant Skinner said, "Doc, we want you to go with us on another little trip next week. Afterwards, you can catch up with your ship in Manila, the Philippines. What do you think?"

"I don't know, sir," I replied. "If I do go, can I carry a BAR this time?"

"Hell no!" chimed Gunny and Sergeant Ryan at the same time, laughing at my request.

"I'll have to check with Chief Beagle, but yes, I'd like to go with you," I confidently said.

"You won't have to check with anyone, Doc. It's all been taken care of before we left Tachikawa. Now, let's go over to Operations, and we'll get this gig underway."

I knew he didn't mess around, but this really surprised me how quickly this one came about. I guessed that was just the way Lieutenant Skinner worked.

When we entered Operations, Lieutenant Skinner was greeted by another marine lieutenant who escorted us into his office, which had a small conference table. Skinner said, "Lieutenant Gordon, meet Hospital Corpsman Third Class Lawrence Gentry. You know Potter and Ryan."

"Welcome aboard, Corpsman Gentry. Glad to have another regular member on our team."

Wow, I thought. *Now I'm a regular member of the recon team.* "Thank you, sir, glad to be here."

Lieutenant Skinner said, "As you know, Doc also has Top Security Clearance, and we would like for him to be in on this session, since he is already here. His ship is a couple weeks out, and he is tagging along with us."

"That's fine. Here is the map of the DMZ. You'll be traveling less than fifty miles up on this one, just past Kaesong. There are two more ammo depots that shouldn't be this close to the border, according to the truce. The North Koreans have denied their existence, so it's up to you to make their words come true. I'm sure they'll be well protected, so our work is cut out for us. It's a shame we can't just drop two or three bombs, but we know that can't happen. You'll be flown back to South Korea on Thursday afternoon, and you'll do the helicopter thing again, but this time, from land at 0200 Friday. So, you have two days to prepare."

After about an hour discussing the logistics of the mission, we were ready to leave. "That sounds good, Lieutenant, I will go on over to see the master sergeant and arrange for the other eight men for our team. There will be a couple changes this time. Corporal Johnson and Private Smith won't be ready in time, and we'll need the other replacements. If you'll show Doc to the barracks, Ryan, and get him settled in, Gunny and I will go see Sergeant Greeson."

CHAPTER 2

KAESONG

Sergeant Ryan showed me to the barracks, and we checked in at the duty desk just before 1600 hours. The corporal behind it told Ryan that our group would be in the east wing, and he motioned for a private to direct us to our bunks. The private led us down two corridors; and then, "This is the east wing. Sergeant, you will be in Room E105, and Corpsman, you will be in E107. There is a head between the two rooms. Have a good evening."

We found our rooms, and Ryan paused a moment. "This is usually reserved for visiting officers, so make yourself comfortable. I won't tell anyone you're pretending to be an admiral," he laughed as we opened our doors. "This area is away from the enlisted barracks. None of us have our ranks on our uniforms so you won't get a second glance. Take a few minutes to relax, write a letter home using your ship's address, and I will knock on your door when it's time for us to chow down."

The uniforms issued to us to wear on these top secret missions did not have insignia, chevrons, or badges of rank affixed to them. We were also issued dog tags with assumed names, and we carried no other identification on our persons.

"Thanks, Sarge," I said and went into my carpeted room with the single bed, dresser, and desk. It was small but very comfortable. There was stationery and a pen on the desk, so I thought that writing home was a pretty good idea. After a short letter, I decided to try out the bed for a minute or two.

A knock on the door woke me at 1900 hours, and when I opened it, there stood the fearless threesome. "Wake up, Lazy Ass," Lieutenant

Skinner said laughingly. "Let's go over to the Zebra Club and get a steak and a "manly" drink. I'll tell them I was busted back to private and maybe they'll let me in with you three." We strutted out back and there was a Navy sedan at the curb.

"Get in and I'll drive over to the club" said Gunny, "but I don't know who will drive us back." As it turned out, after we had an outstanding meal at the base's club for enlisted men and just a couple mixed drinks, we had to walk back to the barracks. The sedan was gone. Gunny just laughed and said, "I don't know whose car that was, but they shouldn't have left the keys in it."

"I don't know what you're talking about, Gunny; I never saw a gray Navy sedan with a two-star plate on the front. It's a mystery to me," said the lieutenant. "Anyway, we've got to get a good night's sleep tonight and check out some gear tomorrow morning. We've got business to take care of, gents." The cool March air was sobering as we walked back to our quarters.

I still don't know if that really was the admiral's car or if they were just putting me on as the low man on the totem pole.

After that good night's sleep, we got up at 0530 hours and prepared for a long day. Sergeant Ryan, Gunny, and I went to the mess hall for breakfast. At 0630 hours, we met Lieutenant Skinner at Operations and went back into Lieutenant Gordon's office. "We've got your team all lined up, Lieutenant Skinner," said Gordon. "They will be across the compound with the master sergeant at 0700. You have four new men for this trip, but you know them all, Lieutenant."

"Thanks, Lieutenant Gordon. Will you be coming with us this time? We need someone with your experience."

"No, as much as I would like to, I have to hold this desk down. You guys have a good trip."

With that, we walked the 200 yards across the compound and there sat eight marines that smartly snapped to attention when the lieutenant approached. Mattingly, Sawkowski, Kwan, and Park were there, but the rest of the guys were new to me.

"At ease, men. Good to see you again. Well, *Corporal* Mattingly, I guess we will be expecting more out of a corporal, this trip. Okay, I think all of you know each other except for the doc. This is Hospital Corpsman Lawrence Gentry. 'Doc' Gentry, meet Corporal Reeves and Privates Edwards, McMartin and Grayson. He will take care of you so you had damn well better take care of him. Come inside and Master

Sergeant Greeson will see that we get our gear." We all shook hands and greeted each other.

We were led to the supply room. Our backpacks, ponchos and other gear were stacked along the wall. "Now go to the supply window there and draw your fatigues, boots, socks, long johns, and skivvies in your size. Get it packed up, and we'll get out of here and pick up our hardware. Another change—we're going to fly on ahead today. That'll give us more planning and training time, which we have been short on in the past."

After we picked up our weapons and ammunition, we boarded a bus for the ride back to Tachikawa, just outside Tokyo, for the flight to Korea. We had the bus to ourselves, so Gunny used the time, standing in the middle of the bus with everyone grouped around, to give the details of our mission. "There apparently are photographs of two compounds, identified by intelligence as ammunition depots, ten miles apart, and both within thirty miles of the DMZ. The officials in North Korea deny the existence of the depots, which surprises no one.

"Ryan, on this trip, we will make only one sojourn to the site. You will plant the explosives and set the timers as you go. We won't have the luxury of exploring our options at these locations. Pick the three men you will take with you before we land today."

Sergeant Ryan replied, "If you don't mind, sir, I've talked with Corporals Sawkowski and Mattingly, and they have the experience we need. Maybe you can place Corporal Reeves and Private Edwards on the perimeter, just outside the compound as backup—the rest of you can keep a lookout from the hill behind each depot."

Gunnery Sergeant Potter responded, "I knew you'd have it all figured out, Sergeant. Lieutenant Skinner, do you have anything to add?"

"No, that's got it covered, Gunny. Now let's just sit back, and each of you get with the buddies you will be working with and work out any personal details you have. After this bus ride, there won't be any more *personal details* on this trip." Well, that was clear to everyone that we would not have any arguments or disagreements concerning our duties and assignments.

When we arrived at the airplane, it wasn't an airliner like we had enjoyed on the trip in. There sat an Air Force C-46 ... or C-47, who knows the difference? "Okay, everybody, grab your gear and follow me," yelled the Gunny. "This is how we did it in WW2; you've never had it so good. It sure beats walking!" The Gunny made this comment when we started every trip on an old airplane.

As we climbed the ladder into the transport aircraft, we spotted the canvas seats strung along each side of the fuselage. "Where's the stewardess?" Ski asked. Then he said, "But you're right, Gunny, this is still better than walking … I guess."

"Settle down, Gyrenes," the lieutenant barked, this will take three to four hours, so make the best of it." The door slammed shut and we were underway.

It was a rough but otherwise uneventful flight, and we landed just after nightfall. I'm not really sure where we were, but it was not a very large airfield. We taxied up to a small building that was all there was to pass for a terminal. We saw a few small planes and several helicopters. When I saw the marine Sikorsky HRS-1 helicopters, I knew what they were for. I think the marines called it "Tactical Redeployment." That ain't what most guys called it. Most of the time it was sending us back into combat or "You marines go first – we'll be right behind you!" Yeah, sure! Way behind us!

"Doc, we'll get a jeep to take you down to a Unit five miles down the road, and you can draw your medical packs and whatever else you need," said Lieutenant Skinner. "So far, everyone is in good shape and ready to go, and we'll be in those tents over behind the mess hall there."

I got into the jeep a few minutes later and drove on down to a field hospital at a marine encampment. There were probably thirty four-man tents set up and four hospital tents. I went into what looked like the main tent and heard, "Doc, what the hell are you doing here?" It was Corpsman Lanny Young from South Carolina, whom I had gone to Great Lakes Hospital Corps School with. "I haven't seen you since Great Lakes. What have you been up to?"

"Just pounding the ground with a bunch of gyrenes!" I said. I couldn't believe I had run into Young, of all people. He was one of my best friends. We had studied together many hours while in corps school. We spent twenty or thirty minutes together reminiscing when I told him I was there to pick up a couple field medical packs. "I was told someone would be picking up these combat packs, but I didn't expect it to be you. You're not the one going with that recon team to Kaesong, are you?"

"I don't know what you're talking about, man. I just needed a few supplies," I replied.

"That's what I thought. Take care of yourself. Maybe we can catch up on things when you get back."

"I hope so. See ya' in a few days."

I got back to the airstrip and found the team getting ready to hit the chow tent. We all stored our gear and secured our rifles in the rack. Corporal Mattingly locked the rifle rack, and we were ready to chow down. We got to the chow tent just as the other marines were finishing up. Several guys recognized buddies they had been stationed with, but very little was said. So the reunions were left for another day. After a good meal, Gunny got us all back to our tents and said reveille would be at 0400 hours. A quick shower and early to bed was the order of the day.

After reveille, we had a quick breakfast, and Lieutenant Skinner led us on a five-mile jog, which ended up right back at the airstrip. "We just need to loosen up the muscles and wipe out the cobwebs. Now everyone, come over to the first tent, and we'll have a little planning session."

The lieutenant went over the details of the mission with everyone together for the first time. There was no one on this trip who had not been on one before. This mission would probably be even shorter than the last one above Pyonggang. Gunny took his turn stressing the buddy system, which everyone had heard since boot camp, but you don't want anyone straying off by himself. Sergeant Ryan took his turn by explaining what types of munitions we would be encountering and which explosives he would be setting and what was expected of us as support.

Lieutenant Skinner gave us all our specific assignments and took us back outside for another short jog. "Now, you have the rest of the day to relax and get all your gear in order. Make sure your rifles and sidepieces are clean and oiled. Get to bed early; you'll hit the deck at midnight and be in the air at 0100 hours."

We headed back to the tent, broke out our gear, and started checking it out. Each man carried a small first-aid pack on his belt that included bandages, tape, powder, and two tubes of morphine with needles so they can medicate themselves until I can get to them. I checked with each man to be sure they had their kits and asked if anyone had any medical needs before we left. I went over to Lieutenant Skinner's tent and asked, "How is that ankle? I noticed you've been limping a little since that jog earlier."

"The ankle's fine, Doc. Thanks for asking; now get some sleep."

At 0045 hours, we loaded into the two helicopters and secured our gear. The blades started slowly rotating, and the engines caught as the blades whirled faster and faster. A few moments later, the 'copters seemed to strain trying to leave the ground, and then we took off in the two birds heading north side by side.

It was dark and cloudy as we flew on, and as we approached the DMZ, the pilots flew as low as they could. After about an hour of zigzagging and changing course, our pilot came on the intercom, "Lieutenant, you are now one mile due south of your objective. We'll be able to get down about ten feet of the deck, so you won't have to rappel as far. Watch your step. Semper Fi."

"Semper Fi!"

The yellow warning lights came on, and ten seconds later, the green light flashed. "*Go, go, go!*" someone shouted, and we went down the rope and hit the deck quickly, getting out of the way before the next boots landed on top of us. The 'copters circled us over the top of the hill and then made their way back the way we'd come.

"Okay, give me a count, Gunny," the lieutenant said quietly.

"Twelve accounted for and all ready to go, sir" he replied.

"All right, Gunny, lead us out."

We started down the hill in the dark night. It was eerie how quiet the surrounding countryside was. There were no lights visible, so we felt confident that we'd made it in without disturbing the North Koreans. It took nearly an hour to reach a spot overlooking the first objective as the moon began to shine through the clouds. Below us was a barbed wire–enclosed compound with several sheds about the size of four carports each.

There were still no lights visible, but we could see a small pickup truck sitting right in front of the gate. We couldn't tell if there was anyone in the truck however. Sergeant Ryan used the scope on his sniper rifle to look around the compound. About that time, two men got out of the truck and lit up cigarettes. They walked up and down by the fence and, after they finished the cigarettes, climbed back into the truck.

"Sergeant Ryan, take Ski and Matt with you and get into position in the underbrush, while Reeves and Edwards move ahead and take out the two guards—quietly!"

Sergeant Kwan spoke up. "Sir, what if I approach the truck and call the guards out to get them out of the truck?"

"What if they shoot your ass; then where will we be? Just wait here, and Reeves and Edwards will take care of them. That's what they do." The lieutenant looked around, "Everyone, look alive, and you five move on down the hill. Let's spread out at ten-foot intervals and cover for them."

We could see our men moving through the underbrush. After ten minutes, Reeves and Edwards moved out into the open, forty yards behind the pickup. Crouching low, they moved slowly to each side of the truck. They eased forward, jerked the doors open, and stabbed the guards repeatedly. They gave a thumbs-up to Ryan, and the three demolition men moved to the gate.

Reeves and Edwards spread out and provided cover from that level. Ryan, Ski, and Matt cut the lock on the gate and went from shed to shed throughout the compound. There were six sheds in all and several barrels of gasoline beside one of them. It's amazing how there is always gasoline stored with the ammunition, mortar rounds, hand grenades, and other munitions. Our five team members were halfway back up the hill when the explosions started. One shed after another exploded with a flash in quick sequence. When the explosions started, Ryan and his men cut loose, shooting the barrels, and in a second, the gasoline started exploding. Beautiful! You've never seen anything like it in your life.

As soon as the five had rejoined our group, the lieutenant got us moving down the west side of the hill and away from the exploding shells, which would continue for a good while. It would be dangerous to approach that compound from any direction for several hours. We made it to the next ridge before we heard the sound of engines. Before long, we saw the helicopters circling the compound. They started moving around the surrounding mountains with their spotlights swinging back and forth on the ground below. They were slowly moving south, so we headed west and north toward the next objective. We now saw headlights speeding up the road back down in the valley. We were moving away from them.

Before we got to the next ammunition depot, daylight was approaching. We found a cave and Sergeant Kwan and Corporal Park volunteered to check it out. Using their flashlights, the two Koreans started inside, and Kwan called back to us, "There's a turn about twenty feet ahead." They moved out of sight.

Then, Park stuck his head around the bend, "Come on in, there's a room back here large enough for us all."

The lieutenant told McMartin and Grayson to stay near the entrance, and the rest of us went on into the damp, musty room in the back of the cave. There were no other exits visible.

"I can't believe there isn't another door from this room," Corporal Park said. "There should be another way out of here." We searched all around the room with our bayonets and shined our flashlights all around but that was it.

Gunny Potter set a watch schedule, and we all claimed a spot around the wall of the space. After we ate our rations, Reeves and Edwards spelled the two privates at the entrance, so they could get something to eat. It was nearly full daylight, and we could hear helicopters in the distance. The lieutenant and the gunny eased out of the entrance and looked around the mountainside. There was nothing in sight down the valley, and they returned back inside. "It's not going to stay this quiet, so let's get some rest, because there's no way we can go out in this daylight," said the lieutenant.

We all lay back and tried to relax. We did get a little sleep, and around noon, we heard helicopters getting louder and louder.

"We won't go out the mouth of the cave in the daylight unless we have to. We can see most of the valley from here. Sergeant Kwan, I've been thinking about what you said about another outlet from the cave. Let's go back in there and take another look," said Lieutenant Skinner.

Everyone except the two on watch went back into the cavern and looked around, high and low with our flashlights, and jabbing into the wall with our bayonets. Corporal Park, the shortest man on the team, called the lieutenant over and told him to look at a spot just over his head. We all shined our lights to the area as he started probing with his bayonet, and it sunk into the soil.

"Good job, Corporal," he said. "This is it." Skinner swung his bayonet back and forth and then started digging deeply into the wall until he found two, upright ten-inch boards with the soil packed tightly over them. A couple of the guys removed the boards while we covered them with our weapons. Inside the smaller tunnel, we could see brush had been piled in to conceal the entrance.

"Pull the brush back this way so we won't disturb anything on the outside." Corporal Park crawled into the opening, handing back brush until he reached the mouth about ten feet from the new opening. "I can see a longer distance to the right from here," he reported. That meant we had a much larger view of the outside world. There was room for two men to watch what was happening, so Gunny set another watch schedule to start immediately. Corporal Park and I took the first watch in the small tunnel.

We could hear the helicopters, and it sounded as if they had passed on by this location, but I was sure they would be back. There was very little underbrush and very few trees to be seen on the surrounding mountainside. It seemed we would be here until after dusk today for sure. "This is one time I want to get out and get moving," I heard Gunny say. "I feel like we're trapped and can't get out."

"Well, that's about the way it is, Gunny, but we'll be out of here in about four or five hours," replied the lieutenant.

The afternoon was uneventful, thank goodness, except for the helicopter flying around about once an hour. It was getting dark, and we gathered our gear together after finishing off another round of rations. We dug a pit, buried all our trash and leftovers, and used a brush to sweep the floor to remove our footprints. The team gathered outside the cave and verified our compass bearings; then we headed out around the hill. It had been about forty-five minutes since we last heard a helicopter, so based on the schedule they'd kept all day long, we had about fifteen minutes to get to the trees up ahead. We made it to the tree line; there was not a sound of the 'copter in the night air.

The gunny turned us downhill, "Let's go to the valley between those two hills; it should be easier and faster walking. We are less than two miles from our next happy hour."

The walking was easier and faster, but it seemed almost too easy—we weren't used to moving this fast on a trip. After an hour of walking and pausing occasionally to listen, we started up a hill. Gunny let us know that we needed to get to the top so we could see the alleged ammo dump. When we topped the hill, we crouched behind some underbrush and were surprised to see that the ammunition depot was all lit up. There were a dozen trucks and probably fifty men walking around inside the compound. There were eight or ten sheds similar to those at the last dump. There was what looked like gasoline barrels stacked on the left side of the sheds and another stack in the front center of the buildings.

"I couldn't have designed this any better for an ambush," whispered Sergeant Ryan. "They have the place lit up like a Christmas tree, the gas barrels are stacked in the best spots, and the men are all inside barbed wire. Lieutenant, we've got to do this in a hurry. Ski can train the BAR on the center-front stack of barrels; Mattingly and Reeves mount the grenade launchers on the Garands; Ryan hit the stack of barrels on the left with tracers in your 03; and the rest of us can open up with our rifles. Starting at the front gate and work your way back."

"Great plan, Sergeant. Does anyone have any questions on what you are going to do? I didn't think so. Spread out and get into position behind those rocks. In one minute, I will start firing and you follow. Take aim carefully, squeeze them off, and don't let up! Get in place."

"Let 'er rip!" All hell broke loose. I was concentrating on men near the front gate. They were running back and forth and dropping like flies. I was suddenly aware of the sound of the BAR to my right above everything else, and then the gasoline barrels started exploding. The grenades exploded in the compound when ammunition and larger shells in one of the sheds started going off from the gasoline fire. The gasoline on the left blazed up and exploded from Sergeant Ryan's tracers. We kept firing, and in rapid succession, the other sheds started burning and exploding ammunition, hand grenades, mortar rounds, and whatever else was flying all over the place.

"Cease fire, cease fire! Hold it a minute and scope this place out," said Lieutenant Skinner. "Do you see anyone moving? Ryan, if you see anyone take them out. You've got the scope."

Ryan fired a couple rounds and said, "If anyone's left, they won't last long. It's getting hotter and hotter down there. Nobody's going to believe this one."

The explosions kept getting louder and larger. "We better get out of here before it starts getting hot up here on us," said the gunny. "Let's head southwest from here and move as fast as we dare. These woods are going to be crawling with North Koreans before you know it."

I didn't say anything about it, but nobody had gotten so much as a scratch.

We moved down the hill opposite to the side we had come up, so we could move away from both objectives and run less of a chance of running into enemy soldiers. We walked as fast as possible, stopping from time to time to listen to the sounds of the night. The moon came out brightly, and it was like daylight around us. "Keep moving, men. We can't stop here and try to hide from anyone because of a little moonlight," said the gunny. Fifteen minutes later, the moon went behind the clouds, and it started raining like crazy.

"Thank you, God," said Lieutenant Skinner. "It might be rougher going, but it will make us harder to spot. Break out your ponchos and keep moving."

About two miles down the trail, Gunny took us south toward home. It would take us about two full nights, maybe three, to get back to our civilization. We could still hear an occasional blast behind us. There were still no sounds of anyone coming our way. *Just keep walking*, I kept telling myself. It was getting harder, but then … we walked right into it.

All of a sudden, gunshots rang out and bullets began whizzing all around us. The flashes in the bushes were straight ahead. "Get down and spread out!" yelled Lieutenant Skinner. We returned fire immediately. Corporal Sawkowski's BAR was raking the bushes left and right. Every time I saw a flash, I would shoot at that spot, as did everyone else. Then a grenade was tossed into the bushes. After a few minutes—or was it an eternity?—the incoming fire ceased.

"Hold it!" Gunny yelled. "Keep it down a minute." After twenty or thirty seconds, he moved forward slowly motioning for a couple of men to circle around each flank. They found four North Korean soldiers lying side by side. We had taken them out. I started looking around and couldn't find everyone.

"Doc, come over here," said Lieutenant Skinner. "I'm hit in the left arm, but see about the others. This is just a flesh wound."

I found Corporal Mattingly and Private McMartin next to each other, and they weren't moving. I checked both of them. There wasn't any pulse. Before I said anything, I shined a light on them, and their wounds confirmed my findings. "Gunny, look over here. Matt and McMartin didn't make it. You better take a head count," I said quietly. I moved on over to the lieutenant and reported the casualties to him as I cleaned and dressed his wound. It was clean through and through. "I'll take a better look at it in the daylight. Do you want a shot?"

"No, sir," he replied. "Not tonight. We need to get them up the hill and off this trail, and we'll find a spot for Matt and Mac."

The gunny came over and told the lieutenant that the other ten were alive and accounted for.

We climbed for about ten minutes and found a fairly level spot with a couple trees on it. "This will be the best place for them that we'll find tonight," said Lieutenant Skinner. We started digging the two graves, taking turns so each of us helped take care of our brothers. The lieutenant led a brief service praising the two men and recited two bible verses. He then led us in prayer, ending with the Lord's Prayer. "Okay, Gunny," he said, "you know the drill. Mark the location on two maps, one for me and give the other to the doc."

"Yes, sir. Okay, men, it's time to move on around this hill and up the next one. Keep your eyes and ears open. Move out."

Miles and hours later, we'd stopped twice, but no one had anything to say. It was hard traveling, but we reluctantly moved on, leaving our two brothers behind. Nothing worse! We moved on until near daylight, and the rain hadn't stopped. It was getting colder and colder. The rain was starting to freeze on the bushes.

"It's not winter time yet," Ryan complained.

"It might not be, but it sure feels like it," said Ski. "Let's find a place to hole up before it gets too light." It was already 0715, but the clouds kept us covered.

"Over there is a rock ledge near the ridge. We have a good view of the whole mountainside and the valley from here. Come on up here, men," said the lieutenant.

"Looks great," replied the gunny.

"Lieutenant, I need to take a look at that arm while I can see what I'm doing," I said, taking him by the arm and sitting him down." The wound looked pretty good. I removed a little debris with tweezers and forceps on both sides of his arm and dusted it good with sulfa powder. I then applied a moist Bactine patch to each side and bandaged the wound. "I should have run a stick through it to make sure we had everything cleaned out, but that will do for now."

"You would like that, wouldn't you?" said the lieutenant.

"Just kidding, sir, just kidding."

We got our backs up under the ledge, covered up with our ponchos, and pulled out our rations. Anything would taste good now; hot coffee would be better, but … "After you get something to eat, guys," I said to them all, "don't forget to pull off those boots for a few minutes and put on some dry socks and use the powder."

"Okay, okay, Doc," everyone responded. "We heard you." I just smiled.

It took me thirty minutes for that same little chore; my fingers were about numb. I hadn't even realized it until I started to untie my shoelaces. We all sat back as close to each other as we could, to stay warm. Ryan and Kwan took the first watch, as they most usually did.

I woke up and started to move. "Doc, if you move I'll kill you with my bare hands. This is the first time I've been this warm in three days," Gunny barked. The rain had frozen over us and the body heat had built up under the ponchos. It wasn't really bad. The wind couldn't get to us through the ice. Ryan came over and got Reeves and Edwards to take the next watch.

"Okay, keep it quiet, men. Stay as dry and warm as you can. We will move out at 1700," the lieutenant said. We stretched our legs and got back up under the ledges.

"I heard helicopters three times since we've been here; they haven't forgotten about us," added the gunny. I hadn't thought he'd been asleep all that time.

"They came around four times—you missed one. Don't tell me you went to sleep, Gunny," said Sergeant Ryan. Everyone grinned at that one.

Everyone woke up some time after 1600 hours. We had been cramped up under the ledges long enough. "Stretch 'em out and get ready to go. Go ahead—eat. Then get your gear together," said the gunny.

"Gunny, I've found a small spring of water over here in this rock cluster. It may be rainwater, but it tastes good," Corporal Park said.

"Okay, everyone fill your canteens and get a good drink of water at the same time."

The rain had slackened, but it was still cloudy and not quite as cold. It actually felt good to move out and start walking. It seemed everyone let out a sigh of relief to be on the move again. It was light enough for us to see where we were going, but dark enough that we felt safe to be out in the open. After about two hours, Lieutenant Skinner motioned us over into the trees and pointed just ahead to a paved highway. It was about a hundred feet lower than we were, and we couldn't hear any traffic.

"Corporal Reeves, you and Private Grayson ease your way on down to the road and let me know what you can see from either direction," said Lieutenant Skinner. We couldn't see to the left or right because of the trees. We watched them as they approached the road, looked both ways, then motioned for us to come on down. They backed off the road until we got down to them. According to the map, we needed to cross the road and head on down the hill to the valley that would lead us to the border. We did that and then heard what sounded like several large trucks.

"Keep your eyes open, people. We'll come within a few feet of that same road near the bottom of the hill," cautioned Gunny.

In a few minutes, Corporal Park held up his hand from the point position where he led the patrol through his familiar home territory and motioned for the lieutenant to come forward. Skinner pointed through the trees to a truck sitting on the highway with his lights off. "They're stopping trucks on the road at various intervals so they can look out for us," said the lieutenant. "Turn around for twenty or thirty yards to that little trail down the hill. We can skirt around them at this location and get on down into the valley, away from the highway." He had wanted to follow the road for a couple more miles, but that was out of the question now.

The team moved through the trees in the valley for about an hour, when Corporal Park stopped us. "We're in *my* area now. My grandfather lives in a village ahead in the next clearing. He will not be able to arrange a ride for us, but if you wait for me here, I can get us some food."

That sounded great to us. "Drop it here, men," said the lieutenant. "I could use some rest and *anything* to eat." We all leaned back against trees, but it was still too wet to sit down. Sergeant Kwan went with Corporal Park to help him carry the food back. I made the rounds, checking on everyone, and most of them asked for a couple APCs for their aches and pains.

It was 2130 hours when we saw Kwan and Park coming through the trees with two figures carrying a large pot. There was another person with them, and as they got closer, Park introduced his elderly, stooped grandfather to us. Park said he was over eighty-five years old and had lived in this village all his life.

Park called us around the pot, "Get your canteen cups, and have some chicken-vegetable soup. My grandfather put it together from two or three pots in the village." It was delicious! Nonetheless, after two or three cups each, there was still half of it left for them to take back to their village. "My grandfather said the soldiers had been to their village two times this week, but no one had seen anything. You don't have to worry about them, they won't tell about us being here. He also gave me directions back to the border that will keep us further away from Kaesong."

Lieutenant Skinner shook hands with Park's grandfather, bowed, and thanked him for his generous hospitality. We started walking around the village and found the trail he had said would be better for us.

We were a little sluggish after the warm meal, but it had raised our spirits tremendously. The lieutenant kept us walking for about two hours. We took a break at 2400 in the edge of a wooded area. The terrain wasn't too bad, except for the muddy spots in the lower areas. The sound of the trucks would get louder at times, but we never seemed to get within half a mile of the highway. I checked with each man, and they all were ready to get back to civilization—such as it was.

At 0230 hours, we took another rest stop for a breath and a drink of water. "Gunny, what's our location now?" asked the lieutenant. "It seems like we ought to be there."

"That's what my kids always say. According to these landmarks, we should be right on this knoll and that puts us four or five hours from the border," said the gunny, pointing to a spot on the aerial photograph that served as our map.

"It's getting better all the time. I believe I can run the rest of the way," kidded Sergeant Ryan.

"Go ahead, Sarge," said the lieutenant, "save us a place at the dinner table."

"Well, I better not show the rest of you up," he replied. "I'll just walk on with you guys."

As we made our way toward the border, the helicopter traffic started to increase. We didn't know if we were still their target, but we ducked into the trees every time we would hear one coming over. At about 0445, we saw a troop truck ahead sitting on the road right in our path. "Stay here under these trees," said Lieutenant Skinner. "We'll just have to wait them out."

We dropped our ponchos onto the ground and lay down on them. We watched the truck until 0530, when they started it and moved down the highway. "All right, men, let's load up and move out," said Lieutenant Skinner. "We'll play their game and keep moving as long as we can. I'm sure we can out think them."

The walk was getting exciting again. We were watching in all directions as we ran across the highway one at a time. This should be the last time we would have to cross this one. Another helicopter flew from west to east about a mile ahead. The sky was starting to brighten, and it looked like we would have a clear sky at sunrise. "We may not make it till tonight, sir," said Kwan to Lieutenant Skinner.

"I know," he replied.

We moved ahead swiftly as we made our way south. Walking through trees, you can see a lot of shadows that look like anything your imagination thinks they might be. None of the imaginary shadows had shot at us yet. After thirty or forty minutes, Park called us to a halt again with his raised hand. "Lieutenant, look right over there. Let me go over and take a look at that truck and see if there's anyone with it and how many there are."

"Take Kwan and Reeves with you and be careful. If it looks like there are more than two or three, just leave them alone and come on back."

"Yes, sir," he said, and they crept the fifty yards to the parked truck. We could see at least one person walk around to the other side of the truck. In about fifteen minutes, we saw our men creep up to the truck. We heard one muffled yelp, and all was silent.

The rest of our team moved through the brush to the truck. "There were only two of them," said Kwan. "We can load up now. Park and I will drive and sit up front; I know the road. We borrowed a couple North Korean jackets, so you men get in the back—let's go home."

The truck hummed down the road. It wasn't paved, but it wasn't very bumpy either. There must have been a lot of traffic on it at one time. We met several other vehicles over the next hour, and then we heard Corporal Park say, "There's the border." He slowed down as if he were going to stop.

Sergeant Kwan stuck his head through the curtain and told us, "Put your heads down; we're not stopping." Park put the truck in second gear, revved the engine, and floored the gas pedal. The guards were caught completely by surprise, and we burst through the border gate at about sixty miles an hour.

"Don't slow down now—they may start shooting!" said the gunny.

After about ten minutes, we saw US military vehicles approaching. The guards on our side of the gates called our military, I'm sure. Corporal Park slowed to a stop, and two US Army trucks pulled up beside us. We all started piling out as the MPs surrounded us.

"Look at this North Korean truck we found up the road on this side of the border," lied Lieutenant Skinner.

The MP corporal said, "That truck burst through the DMZ gate like a bat out of hell and knocked down two North Korean soldiers."

"I don't know what you're talking about, Corporal. I'm Lieutenant

Skinner of the United States marine Corps. Just take us down to the US Marine compound north of Tongduchon, and they'll verify who we are. *We* didn't see anyone break through that damned gate. We saw this abandoned truck and got a free ride. We've been walking for days, and that truck was mighty inviting."

The MP didn't know exactly what to say, but a corporal from the other American truck came over and told him he'd better do what the marine officer said.

"That's the best decision you've made in your whole glorious career," Lieutenant Skinner said loudly. We all got back into the truck and followed one MP truck while the other one followed us down the road to the marine camp.

When we arrived at the airstrip we had left by helicopter a few days ago, there were four or five marines out front. The first one to come over was Lieutenant Gordon from Yokohama. "It's about time you guys got back. You were supposed to return from that training exercise yesterday," he said. Then he turned to the MPs and asked, "Is there a problem, Corporal?"

"These marines were in a North Korean truck that reportedly crashed through the DMZ gate, and this marine lieutenant said they found it abandoned along the road and borrowed it for a ride back here," said the army corporal.

Lieutenant Gordon looked him straight in the face, "If the lieutenant says he found this damned piece of junk abandoned, then I suggest you believe every last word. And by the way, when you leave, take this misplaced truck with you!"

All we heard from the army corporal was a faint, "Yes, sir!" Then they loaded up, and all three trucks were gone as fast as they could scratch out of the camp.

"Lieutenant Gordon, what in the world are you doing here?" asked Lieutenant Skinner.

"I was sent here when Headquarters got a complaint from North Korea that our military had blown up two of their military camps, with the claim they had killed all twenty-five of our 'mercenaries.' We didn't expect *any* of you back this time, but we came just in case."

Gunny quickly said, "I'll bet they thought there were twenty-five of us, but we did leave two buried this time."

"That's right. We lost Mattingly and McMartin," said Lieutenant Skinner, "and they were not military camps, they were—emphasis on *were*—ammunition dumps, and they both lit up the sky like the Fourth of July. I'll bet that ammo is still popping off."

"Get everyone fed and cleaned up. Debriefing is going to be really interesting this trip," said Gordon.

I was hoping to get out of it, but no such luck. They would include the marines, the corpsman, as well as the South Koreans. "Doc, if we could get you out tonight, you could catch your ship in Yokohama tomorrow, but I think you had better catch it in a few days in Manila."

"Thank you, Lieutenant Gordon. I'm sure that will be the easiest course." Then Lieutenant Skinner and I turned the maps marking the graves and their dog tags over to Lieutenant Gordon.

We went to the chow hall first and had a hastily prepared breakfast in midmorning. They took us over to Supply to get a change of clothing and some toilet articles. Then back to our tents. We had until 1300 hours to shower, shave, and whatever, and then to report to the duty hut with all our gear and weapons. There were just five shower stalls available for us, but it didn't take long to work out that little problem.

At 1300, we walked over to the duty hut, and Lieutenant Gordon told us to bring our gear over to the trucks. There were three marines there with clipboards, and they checked off our gear and weapons and loaded them onto the trucks. "Okay," a marine said smiling, "does anyone have any souvenirs? You have to turn everything in." Everyone laughed and we held our hands out, turning them over back and forth. "You know I have to ask. Now everyone, right over there we have a C-47 that I think you're familiar with. So, go back to your tents and have a good afternoon, then get a good night's sleep. Reveille at 0530; chow down at 0600; and be at the airstrip at 0700. Semper Fi, gentlemen."

"Semper Fi, sir," we replied. I tried to get in touch with Corpsman Young, but it didn't work out.

At 0700 hours, the C-47 taxied to the end of the airstrip, turned, and roared down the runway. We were airborne on the way back to Tachikawa. I guessed that's where we were headed—no one said for sure. The bumpy ride in the canvas sling seats was actually a little better than the ride in the back of that truck we crashed through the gate yesterday morning. I brought that up, and the vote was close in favor of the C-47. After about three and a half or four hours, we landed at Tachikawa, Japan.

Again, we were met at the plane by a bus. When we boarded the bus, there was Captain Blakenship who had been in charge of our debriefing last trip. "Welcome, gentlemen. We're going to start your debriefing process in one hour. We'll stop by the mess hall. We have a section reserved for you, and then we'll go over to the administration building and get started." We went through the chow line and were directed to a section of tables by MPs. Did they think we were going to blow up the chow hall? Who knows, but after a quick meal, we were bused over to Administration.

Captain Blakenship led us to the conference room. "All of you've been through this process before. Answer the questions as we ask them, and offer no other information. You will not ask us questions. We'll now call your names, and you'll go with the debriefing officer assigned to you. None of you will have the same officer that interviewed you before. Lieutenant Skinner, just stand by, I'll be interviewing you myself. Gunnery Sergeant Potter, you go with First Lieutenant Smith …" And so on down the line it went.

My debriefing officer was a Second Lieutenant Barstow, who showed me to an office and closed the door. "You'll answer the questions as I ask them so let's get started. Were you the medical support for the recon team that went into North Korea this past Thursday?"

"No sir. I don't know what you are talking about," I answered with a smile.

"Okay, Corpsman—"

Then I quickly answered, "Yes, sir, I was."

"That's more like it. You can talk to me." This went on for over an hour, and he thanked me for my cooperation. "Good luck, Corpsman. Here's twenty dollars spending money, since you're not allowed to bring anything with you. Now we'll go back to the conference room." It all went pretty much as it did the first time, but Lieutenant Barstow didn't shake hands.

I spent two more nights at Tachikawa, and the other team members left for their respective permanent assignments. They flew me to the Philippines, and I was bused over to the naval station in Manila. There I would wait for two days until my ship arrived, and we would sail back to San Francisco, California. I was back in the navy again.

CHAPTER 3

SARIWON

The trip back to San Francisco from Manila was quite enjoyable. The weather was good. I got to sleep in a bunk at night. And the food was great. The food aboard the ship was always good, but it just seemed better now for some reason. There were 3,800 US Army infantry aboard the ship on this trip, so our infirmary was always busy, needless to say. The soldiers had as many shipboard injuries as the marines had mentioned before.

The Golden Gate Bridge looked great spanning the San Francisco Bay as we sailed under it, docking at the Fort Mason Pier. It took only two hours for the troops to disembark and for the ship's company to secure the ship. We didn't have to keep any corpsman on board when the ship was in it's home port. There is medical care available nearby on shore.

After four days in San Francisco, we were back on the ship, preparing for a trip back to Yokohoma, Japan, with brief stops in Honolulu and Okinawa. There were to be 3,600 marines and military dependents on this trip. There were two new corpsmen added to our complement, so we would have some extra help on this voyage. I wondered if they were looking for my replacement, since I had been used on temporary assignments in Korea so frequently.

The ship backed away from the Fort Mason Pier into the bay and headed back out under the Golden Gate Bridge. This was going to be my seventh voyage across the Pacific Ocean. I had been to Hawaii, Guam, Kwajalein, Okinawa, the Philippines, Formosa, Korea, and Japan on this ship. My duties aboard ship as a hospital corpsman included care of patients in the sick bay, taking and developing x-rays, holding sick call, and caring for patients in the infirmary. Currently, I was the resident pharmacist. Pharmacist duties included filling prescriptions written by ship's doctors and dentists, compounding elixirs, cough medicines, and maintaining the inventory of medicines. My most boring chore was putting together and filling the little boxes that held eight APC tablets or eight PBZ (Pyrabenzamine antihistamine) cold tablets. I also had to write the contents on literally hundreds of boxes.

This voyage was underway by 1030 hours on a Friday. A common joke in the navy was that the designation USS before the name of a ship stood for "Underway Saturday and Sunday." It seemed true enough to us most of the time. The stop in Hawaii was only for a few hours to pick up troops and their dependents being transferred to Japan. The trip to Okinawa just took two or three days and there were more troops picked up to go to Japan. Although these two stops were for just a few hours, there was always time to go ashore long enough for a steak and a beer or two. We alternated shore leaves on these brief visits so everyone got a little time off.

The weather was rainy and quite dreary when the ship docked in Yokohoma. There was a huge crowd awaiting the arrival of the dependents of the servicemen that were already there. They disembarked from the main gangplank. The troops carrying their duffle bags disembarked from the aft gangplank and loaded onto the waiting trucks.

After all the passengers were safely ashore and the ship was secured, the crewmembers with passes prepared to go ashore.

"Doc, you have a visitor," I heard from the passageway outside our stateroom.

"Huh? Oh," I thought, "I know who that is." Yep, there stood the gunny. "I knew it would be one of you guys," I said as we shook hands, and then he gave me a big bear hug, which I didn't expect.

"I thought you'd be on the main deck waiting on me, Doc. Now I see why you like this ship and that bed. I know how you like the outdoors and all that hiking."

To which I replied, "I was right; I guess this is not a social call. Who do we need to talk with to discuss *this* shore leave?"

"You know the lieutenant better than that, Doc. You were cleared for this two days ago," he said. "Lieutenant Skinner is in Lieutenant Gordon's office as we speak, making plans. This one is quite a bit different than any we've tried before. We'll discuss it when we get out of here. Leave everything in your locker that you won't need." Just as before, we wouldn't be taking any money or identification and nothing in our pockets that would clink or rattle.

The chief hospital corpsman came by and confirmed that my temporary duty transfer was approved effective immediately. "Good luck," he said, "we'll probably see you back in San Francisco."

"Thanks, Chief, I don't know yet how long this will take. I have locked my valuables in the pharmacy safe, just so you know," I replied. The chief and the doctor were the only others with the combination to the safe.

"Thanks for letting me know; we'll have steaks all around tonight," he said jokingly—I hoped.

Gunny Potter drove me to Lieutenant Gordon's office in a Navy Suburban. "You didn't borrow this vehicle from the admiral, did you, Gunny?" I asked.

"No, Doc; I checked this one out in my name. This one isn't borrowed," he replied.

"So, you admit you borrowed that sedan from the admiral," I chided him.

"I don't admit nothin' about nothin', and you know it."

"Well, I was just checking!" *Enough of that*, I thought, *I'd better not get him all riled up*. We walked into the office, and Gunny said, "I don't know if we want this guy with us this time or not. He's been back at sea too long and nothing but a wise ass."

Everyone laughed, and I said, "I don't know what he's talking about."

I looked at Lieutenant Gordon, but he now had "railroad tracks" on his collar. He was now *Captain* Gordon.

"Congratulations, sir," I said, "and hello to you, too, Lieutenant Skinner."

"Thanks, Doc, we've all said hello now, so we've got a lot to discuss," said the captain. "Gunny, call Ryan and the other team members in here; they need to be in on this."

"Aye, aye, Captain," replied Gunny.

Ryan, Sawkowski, Reeves, Edwards, and Grayson came in and shook hands with me, and we all sat down. "This mission is entirely different from anything we've done before." said Captain Gordon. "We have reports that there may be fifteen to twenty American POWs in a small camp outside Sariwon, North Korea. That's fifty miles south of Pyongyang and sixty miles inland from the Korea Bay. There's a railroad that runs from Pyongyang down through Sariwon on which we think they transport the POWs. Of course, the North Koreans deny the existence of the POWs, but we have reliable reports from eye witnesses."

Lieutenant Skinner added, "Our orders are to take a team of ten men in on two helicopters, check this out, and bring as many back with us as possible. After the mission is completed and with the help of our Korean friends, three helicopters will meet us at the coast at a predetermined time and place to pick us up and our additional cargo. This will be touch and go, but we're used to operating like that."

"Let's go across the hall to the meeting room," suggested the gunny, "and we can go over the maps and assignments. Are Kwan and Park in on this one, and are they on base?"

Lieutenant Skinner replied, "They'll be here at 0730 tomorrow. All the briefing will be done here in this building, and there will be no contact with any personnel outside of our team after we leave here. Now, let's look at some maps."

We studied the maps for over an hour as the lieutenant and captain explained the logistics until we understood our assignments. "Let's break for dinner and knock off for tonight. Too much knowledge may make some of those heads explode," said the captain. "Gunny has your barracks assignment with all of you staying in the same wing. Remember, you all stay in the same area, eat in the same area, and talk to no one outside the team. We'll meet back here at 0700 and see what you have learned today. Go get something to eat and get some rest."

"Okay, Gyrenes, and you too, Doc. Double file, and we march everywhere we go. Look sharp. Forward, MARCH! Left, right, left …" We were off to the mess hall looking sharp, the marines in their fatigues and me in my dress whites. Sharp!

When we got to the barracks, we found our bunks. Gunny had arranged for fatigues, skivvies, socks, boots, and shaving gear for me. Now I had something to change into and not stand out like a sore thumb. Although we were on a navy base, we were working on the marine compound. I don't know about everyone else, but I had a good night's sleep. A shower and shave the next morning, and I was ready to march to the mess hall and then to the administration building.

At 0700 hours, we were all in the meeting room, except Sergeant Ryan, who was on the way to get Sergeant Kwan and Corporal Park.

The Untold Experiences of a Navy Corpsman

I was glad that we had the same team as before for this mission. The captain started the meeting by explaining what equipment and weapons we each would be responsible for. At 0740, Ryan came in with Kwan and Park. Our ten-man marine Recon Team was all assembled and ready to go. The captain pointed out that Sergeant Ryan had been promoted to staff sergeant and Privates Edwards and Grayson had each made Lance Corporal.

"What about you, Corpsman, have you received a promotion lately?"

"No, I am still *Doc*," I replied.

The first half of the day was spent briefing us on the upcoming mission. Then Gunny took us over to Supply to draw our additional clothing, rations, and supplies. Then to the armory to draw our weapons, ammo, and other munitions. After we were squared away, back to the meeting room for the final briefing. "You'll be bused back up to Tachikawa Air Base this evening and fly out to Seoul, South Korea. Upon arriving in Seoul, there'll be a bus to take you north to your helicopters. If all goes as scheduled, you'll be on the ground before daylight fifteen miles west of Sariwon—further inland than we first anticipated," said the captain. "If the pilot can get closer to the objective, it's his decision. We don't want to get close enough to tip our hand. Good luck, men. I'll be going with you as far as Seoul, so if you have any questions, save them for the airplane ride. Semper Fi!"

"Semper Fi, sir!"

Here we go again. You can bet there will be no beer on this bus. It's all business from here on out. That's the way it should be. We made the familiar bus ride up to Tachikawa and were taken directly to the C-47. We got inside, and it had real seats, two seats on one side and one on the other.

"No canvas seats this trip! What's going on, Lieutenant?"

"Don't ask; they may change their minds. We'll take this one," replied Skinner. "Everyone spread out so you can lean the seats back and get some sleep. We've got the whole plane to ourselves. There are some bag lunches a couple seats back and drinks in the cooler." The captain and the lieutenant took the front seats and we spread out towards the rear of the cabin.

First Class, I thought out loud. It seemed as much.

The plane landed at the airport outside Seoul just before 2400 hours, and there was the drab green unmarked bus waiting on the tarmac.

There was also a sedan for Captain Gordon. We boarded the bus and gave the captain just one more chance to go with us, but he declined saying, "You know, this is one that I really want to go on. I did ask, but was told to take care of business here. Take care of yourselves and bring all those guys back with you!" The bus pulled out, and Captain Gordon waited by his sedan until we were on our way.

The trip from Seoul up to Munsan was only thirty or so miles, but it took over an hour. It was almost on the border with North Korea. We arrived at a small airstrip that had just two small planes and four helicopters that I could see. There were only two tents and no permanent buildings. We got off the bus and were met by two helicopter pilots and a gunnery sergeant who was in charge of the airfield. The pilots asked if we had brought someone else with us as a pair of headlights approached. Then Captain Gordon climbed out of the car. "I just wanted to make sure you got into the air and didn't back out on us," he said.

"I knew you wanted to go with us," Lieutenant Skinner said. Then the captain called the lieutenant and Gunny Potter over and talked in hushed voices for six or eight minutes. Then they called the two pilots over and talked with them for a couple minutes.

Lieutenant Skinner came over and said, "Okay, men, load 'em up. You know which bird you ride in. It's time to get this show on the road." We all climbed into our respective helicopters and settled in for the ride. After we were airborne, the lieutenant said, "Our route has been changed. Instead of going north over the border, we'll fly west first, out over the Yellow Sea, and then north over Korea Bay. The pilots will fly as low as possible back inland and sit us down as near to Sariwon as they can without giving away our position." It occurred to me that the pilots and our team never used the others' names. All part of the game, I guessed.

We were flying inland now, and trees were flying by left and right as we zigzagged over the countryside. Looking down, the terrain was starting to look awfully rough, and we were getting into the mountains. It was now 0300 hours and partly cloudy. *Here we go again*, I thought.

"We can't get much closer, Lieutenant, you're eight miles from your objective at this point. I can't see any bandits from my vantage point," came a voice over the speaker. We started slowing and circling.

"Check your gear and get it ready," Lieutenant Skinner said as the yellow light started flashing. "You'll have to rappel about twenty feet because of the underbrush."

"Have a good trip and be safe!" said the pilot as the green light flashed on. *"Go, go, go ...!"* We hit the ropes and were on the ground getting out of the way of the others.

"Round 'em up and give me a count, Gunny!" said the lieutenant as the helicopters circled and flew out of sight. "Ten accounted for and ready to go, sir," replied Gunny. "According to the compass and maps, we need to go east eight miles from here."

"All right, men. Follow the gunny's direction. Reeves, you'll take the lead position for now, with Corporal Park. Move out."

The moon was partly out, so we could see our surroundings fairly well. There were no lights as far as we could see, and no engine noises could be heard.

The mountains were neither as steep nor as high in this area, and the walking wasn't bad. We were making good time and expected to be in position to see our objective before daylight. The lieutenant called us to a halt for a break. "Now, I'll fill you in on the scuttlebutt. We'll make contact with one of the eyewitnesses, who'll lead us to the location the POWs were last seen working. They're doing repairs on the railroad according to the reports." Skinner handed Kwan a paper and said, "Sergeant Kwan, here's the directions to the contact with his name and password. After we reach this point on the map, you'll follow these instructions and bring him back to this location."

Kwan replied, "Yes sir, but according to this name, it may be a *her* instead of a him. In any case, I will return with our contact."

We moved on for another hour or so. It was becoming daylight as we reached our destination. The Gunny Potter stopped us in a grove of trees near the top of a ridge. It kept us pretty well concealed. There was a small village on the far edge of the valley below and the railroad. Ryan pointed to four or five shacks on the other side of the tracks that he spotted with the scope on his sniper rifle. Sergeant Kwan talked with the lieutenant for about five minutes. Then he walked down the hill and moved north, parallel to the tracks and on out of sight.

We relaxed under the cover of the trees and enjoyed our rations before stretching out on our ponchos and taking a little nap. I had checked with everyone, but no one had any complaints that I could help them with. At about 0915, we heard a whistle from the north side of the trees. After thirty seconds, there was another whistle. Then Corporal Park returned the whistle. "That's Kwan coming back in with our friend."

The lieutenant told us to be alert and watch for them to come in. Sergeant Kwan and a small Korean woman walked through the trees. Edwards and Grayson backtracked the trail to make sure they hadn't been followed. The gunny set four men around the perimeter, while the lieutenant talked with the woman. Corporal Park told the rest of us that she was afraid to talk to all of us. She just wanted to talk to the officer in charge, with Kwan translating for her.

After an hour, she left with Kwan and Park. "She's going to show them where she last saw the POWs a week ago," said Lieutenant Skinner. "Then they'll escort her back to her home outside the village. Her husband and two brothers were killed by the North Koreans because they would not join their army, and according to our sources, she and her family have helped with the rescue of over forty of our men." Then he added, "I don't like the idea of them moving around out there in the daylight, but she said it would be okay right now."

Sergeant Ryan came over and said, "I was scoping out what I could see in the valley, and there are eight men working on the railroad tracks, with two armed guards watching over them. They look like they could be the ones we are looking for."

Lieutenant Skinner replied, "Gunny, set up, so we can watch them all day. Your binoculars may not be as powerful as the scope, but keep tab on them until we can make our move. The rest of you get as much rest as you can." No one wanted to sleep, knowing those men were that close, but we couldn't expose our position in full daylight.

We got through the day with naps here and there as we took turns watching the men working on the railroad. At the end of the day, we documented the two shacks the men had gone into. After they were inside, the guards placed a bar across the door. That's all we needed to know. It was getting pretty dark by 2000 hours, and we were ready to move out.

The best we could determine, there were six guards down there, and they were all inside the two shacks to our left. We had been able to tell there were no windows in the sides of the shacks facing our direction. "Here's how we will approach this," said the lieutenant. "First, I want us to circle around to the far side of the shacks and get an idea of what we are up against. I know she told us there were no windows, but we had better see for ourselves. Then we can split up and go in to rescue our men. We'll go to the back of the shacks that the workers are in and identify them before we take care of the guards. Kwan, you and Park, with Reeves, Edwards, and Grayson will watch the guards' shacks. Sawkowski, set the BAR across the tracks and cover us all. Gunny, Ryan, and Doc will come with me and contact the POWs. Okay, move out!"

We moved slowly down the hill and circled to the right, a hundred yards to the rear of the shacks. They were all dark, except for the one to our right that some of the guards were supposedly in. We could see light coming through the cracks. There weren't any vehicles, so they must travel and get all their supplies by train. The lieutenant moved us a little closer and then told us to move around to our positions. The four of us circled back to the left and crept in behind the buildings on our left. We could hear the North Koreans talking inside their shacks. It sounded as if they were having a good time.

Gunny moved up to one shack and Lieutenant Skinner to the other. Ryan and I held back twenty yards at the ready. We could faintly see that Kwan, Park, Reeves, Edwards, and Grayson were getting into position around the guards' shacks. Gunny took his bayonet, stuck it in between two boards, and pried one back. He whispered into the opening and told the men inside who we were. "Keep it quiet," I heard him whisper. "How many men are being held here?"

I couldn't hear the response but found out later there were eight prisoners here in the two buildings: five Americans and three South Koreans. The lieutenant repeated Gunny's procedure with his bayonet and contacted the men in the other shack, telling them to keep it down until we let them know we were opening their doors.

All of a sudden, shots rang out and we heard, "They know we're here. Watch out! They're coming out of both shacks."

We ran around the shack the prisoners were in, and someone was coming right at us. We shot him, and I heard something to my left. I turned around right into a rifle butt to my mouth. As I fell back, my right hand came across the .38 pistol in my shoulder holster, which I pulled out and fired twice at the figure over me swinging his rifle. He froze in place, and I fired two more shots into his chest. As I rolled over, he fell right where I had fallen. Everything was quiet.

Then Gunny said, "Check all of them. I think we got every one. Sound off all of you people! Where are you?"

"I got hit in the mouth with a rifle butt, and I settled up with him. I've still got all my teeth," I said, "but, I still haven't seen all the guys."

Sergeant Kwan called out, "Come over here and look at Park and Grayson. They've both been hit."

I ran over to Park, and he was hit in the right chest, but I didn't think it hit a lung. Grayson was sitting up and said he was hit in the leg. I told Edwards to put a compress on the wound and tie a tourniquet around it. Corporal Sawkowski came running up carrying the BAR and asked, "Am I too late? I couldn't tell one from the other so I didn't fire a shot."

The lieutenant said, "I'm glad you didn't open up from out there with that thing. We took care of business here. Now, Gunny, let's go open up the prisoners' shacks and see what we have. Reeves and Edwards, you back us up as we open the doors. Bring your lights over here. Ski and Ryan, look out for visitors."

I was still working on Park as Kwan held a light. As I was cleaning the wound, I noted the bullet did not go through his body. I soon found it lodged between two ribs. I removed the bullet and tied off a couple bleeders with Ski's help holding the forceps. It was a small caliber, probably a 9 mm pistol round. I put a compress on the wound and told Kwan to hold it. I then took Kwan's flashlight and soon found another wound in his upper thigh, which was bleeding slightly. I placed a compress and tourniquet on that wound and went back to work on his chest. Park hadn't said a word since I got to him, and he was having trouble keeping his eyes open. I had Kwan talking to him, while I finished the dressing. He then went into convulsions and fell limp. I felt for a pulse and found none. I checked for a heartbeat with my stethoscope, and there was none at all. There was nothing else to be done.

By now, Grayson was starting to hurt quite a bit. I asked him if anyone had given him a shot, and he said he wouldn't let them until I got to him. "Thanks, I appreciate the confidence, but you're going to need this," I said as I gave him a shot of morphine. The bullet had gone through and was little more than a flesh wound, as it turned out.

"I thought I was dying at first," he said "and then I looked over and saw Park." I dressed his wound and got him on his feet at least for a few minutes, went to check on the others, and then gave my report to Lieutenant Skinner.

Grayson hobbled with me over to the shacks where Skinner and Gunny were talking with the POWs. As they had said earlier, there were five American soldiers and three South Korean soldiers. "There were twenty-one Americans in their group last week when they brought these five down here from Pyongyang to work on the railroad tracks," said the lieutenant.

"Lieutenant Skinner, I need to talk with you," I said. He came over and I told him about Park and Grayson.

"Where's Kwan?" he asked.

"He's still over there in that opening with Park. We need to go over there," I said.

"Gunny, come with me and Doc. We need you over here." The gunny walked with us over to where Kwan was holding Park. "I'm sorry, Sergeant, but we have to get on the move. The prisoners said a train usually comes by here first thing each morning. Let us help you with Corporal Park. Doc, go over and talk with the prisoners and see if there is anything they need before we start back. By the way, Doc, how's your jaw?"

"I'm okay," I said.

The prisoners were tired, dirty, and hungry, but none of them had any injuries that needed immediate attention. One of the American soldiers was a medic, so he had helped look after the others while they were prisoners.

Lieutenant Skinner called out, "Get everything and everybody ready to go. We got all out of sorts back there, so get it together. Gunny, we'll get back up to our little camp and take care of business up there. Edwards, help Kwan with Park; and Reeves, give Grayson a hand. No smoking, no lights. Move it out." Before we left, three of the prisoners broke open the tool shed and used pry bars to loosen the rails from the cross ties in three places. That should derail at least one train. The POWs also rounded up the guards' weapons and ammunition.

On the way up the hill, my mouth began hurting like crazy. It was hurting badly when we'd left, but now it was almost like I was hit again. I took out an APC and put it in my mouth and crunched it up so it would start working sooner.

We were a scraggly looking bunch by the time we got back up the mountain to our camp. Ryan led us back into the trees to conceal us from being seen. It was now 0300 hours. The moon was bright, and the air was cool but not too cold. I made the rounds with our team and the "ex-prisoners," as they now called themselves. There were a couple small cuts that didn't take long to bandage, and I passed out the usual amount of APCs. Then I went over to re-examine Park one more time just to be sure, and there was no question. When I reached up to get his dog tags, I noticed some blood on his neck, more than should have been there. I called Ski over with his flashlight, examined the source, and pulled out a small sliver of metal from an artery with my tweezers.

Ski called Lieutenant Skinner and the gunny over, and I told them what I had found. "It looks like a sliver from a ricochet. I've never seen one like this before," I said.

"He was killed by hostile gunfire, and there was nothing anyone could have done to save him," said the lieutenant. Gunny, mark the maps and give them to us. Doc, you have one map and the dog tag. We have to bury him here, but he will be recovered and returned home at a later date."

Again, we assisted on digging the grave for Corporal Park. This time the *ex-prisoners* helped with the digging. "We're all too familiar with this practice," said one of them. The burial was somber as Sergeant Kwan recited a prayer in their native language. Then Lieutenant Skinner conducted a short service that ended with all of us joining in the Lord's Prayer. Sergeant Kwan said he and Park had known each other since they were teenagers.

The lieutenant asked the gunny for a count before we moved out. "Seventeen and ready to go, sir," he replied.

"Okay men, we have to put some miles between us and the railroad. Move out," said Lieutenant Skinner.

We were moving a little slower this time, but we kept it going. Lance Corporal Grayson had to lean on someone occasionally to take some pressure off his leg. We found a stick he could use for a cane. It looked like it had been used as a cane before. I had folded a handkerchief and made a mouth guard to protect my six loose teeth and bruised lips. It felt good to clamp down on it from time to time. I rubbed some Bactine on my lips and gums.

Our guests were in amazingly good shape. They were underweight but appeared to be healthy. An army captain who was in charge of this crew said, "We're more than likely the very healthiest of the group. That's why we were selected for the heavy work on the railroad. We were fed enough to keep us alive, but you wouldn't believe some of the other things that a person will eat if they're hungry enough!"

Gunny said, "You'll soon be well fed, sir. Then we'll see what we can do to rescue your buddies."

"That'll be an accomplishment, Sergeant, but we'll do all we can to help," said the captain.

Back on the trail again, we started looking for a place to stop for the day. We were crossing a small valley when we heard what sounded like a truck engine. We dropped to the deck and waited as it got closer. "Don't anyone move unless I say," Lieutenant Skinner ordered. "It sounds like they'll pass close by, but so far, they're not slowing down."

After a few minutes, two trucks did pass by, and we moved on up to the unpaved roadway. The roadway was less than fifty yards from our location. "It's time to get up that hill, men. That was too close for comfort. It'll be daylight before you know it; now, let's move it," he said.

Within thirty minutes, we were well concealed in a grove of trees and rocks. We could now get some rest and meet the rescued POWs in the light of day. One corporal did have a cut on the calf of his leg that was apparently infected. I removed the bandage with the help of the army medic. "It helps when you have medicine and clean bandages to treat cuts," he said. "I've used torn clothing and anything else we could get our hands on for bandages. The only medicines we had were their aspirin most of the time. Once in a while, we would get a small supply of antiseptics and penicillin."

We cleaned the infected wound with peroxide, and did it ever foam! It was painful for him as I swabbed and cleaned the wound. I applied medication and bandaged it with sterile gauze and wrapped it. "Thanks, Doc," he said with a smile. Just send your bill to my accountant."

"My pleasure, Corporal, glad to help." I then changed the bandage for Corporal Grayson and treated a couple other aches and pains. There were a lot of headaches with this crew.

We kept two men on perimeter watch that day, as usual, and were able to get some sleep. It was amazing and a little upsetting at times how the rescued POWs would be lying on the ground asleep and then jump up in a sweat. We would calm them down as they woke up, and they would soon go back to sleep. It happened at least once with each of them.

As night began to fall, we started to get ready to walk through the night and possibly reach the helicopters before another sunrise came. The lieutenant, Gunny, and Kwan spent a lot of the day talking and going over maps. I didn't ask any questions, and they didn't offer any answers. "Check your gear and weapons. Doc, did you reload that pistol yet? That was a quick reflex," the lieutenant said.

"It's loaded and ready to go. I've just got some sore teeth." I replied.

"Count 'em out, Gunny. Move them out," said Lieutenant Skinner.

"Seventeen on the move, Lieutenant; lead us out of here, Ryan and Kwan. Set a steady pace and keep your eyes open, people," barked the gunny.

We were a little sore and stiff as we started out after lying on the ground, but we got it in gear before long. There was a definite chill in the air now, and the sky was clear. The moon was going to be bright, so we should make pretty good time if we didn't run into any problems. The eight extra men were making a dent in our rations, but that really should be okay since we expected to be back across the border within twenty-four hours. After two hours, we stopped in another grove of trees to rest and grab a drink of water. A couple miles back, we had crossed a stream and refilled our canteens, but it was in the wide open and we couldn't linger there. Grayson asked for a couple APCs for the pain in his leg from the wound. I would check it out at daylight and redress it.. A twenty-minute rest stop was long enough; everyone wanted to get out of there.

At 2400 hours, Kwan raised a hand and motioned us over behind some rocks and underbrush. We were moving out of the mountainous terrain and closer to the smaller hills. He told Lieutenant Skinner, "I hear something up ahead. I don't think we should all move ahead until we check it out."

"Take one man with you and see what you can find," said the lieutenant.

Kwan took Corporal Reeves around to the right and into the shadows and then soon out of sight. They came back in fifteen minutes and both were laughing. There was a jeep up on a roadway with a flat tire. One soldier was sitting in the jeep and the other one was changing the tire while cursing all the time. "I don't know if the one in the jeep was an officer or not, but the other one wasn't happy," said Reeves. We sat back and listened for about another thirty minutes, when we heard voices and then the jeep roared off. "I think they got it fixed," laughed Reeves. Everyone got a chuckle out of the whole episode, and then we started on through the woods, across that road and on down the next hill.

Less than an hour later, Gunny said, "Lieutenant Skinner, the little village up ahead is where our contact is to get us in touch with the helicopters."

The lieutenant called Kwan over and handed him the paper with the name of the contact, his (or her) location, and the passwords. Kwan took Reeves with him again, and they moved across the open area into some trees toward the village. Lieutenant Skinner sat down with Gunny, Ryan, and me and said, "This'll be interesting. He is supposed to send a radio message to his 'grandfather' to pick up the 'grandchildren' for a visit, and he'll need to bring three gifts. That translates that our superiors need to pick us up in three helicopters. Let's see how well that works."

It was 0145 when we saw a flash of light; ten seconds later, there were two flashes. Ryan returned the signal after ten seconds with three flashes, and our men came out into the open with a third figure following them. Kwan and Reeves came on in, and Kwan introduced the man with them to Lieutenant Skinner and Gunny Potter. They talked for five or six minutes, and we heard Gunny say, "Hot *damn*, that's great!"

The lieutenant laughed quietly and said, "I couldn't have said it better myself, Gunny. Grandpa said it would be four days before he could come, but that means he will be here at 0400. Come on everyone, we're going home."

The army captain said, "We've waited over four years to hear that phrase. We're ready to go."

We followed Kwan and our contact back across the opening and then into another wooded area. We followed them for over an hour, and then they stopped us in the shadows. Kwan said, "This is the pick-up area. They will land one at a time in the opening just past the trees. Six men will go to the first 'copter, six in the second, and five in the third one."

Gunny motioned us over and said, "We will put Lieutenant Skinner, Grayson, and four of the POWs in the first bird. Ryan, Reeves, and the other four POWs will go next. Then Ski, Edwards, Kwan, Doc, and I will be in the third one. Break up into the groups now, so there will be no confusion. We don't want anyone left behind."

Lieutenant Skinner went over to our contact and thanked him for his loyalty and his assistance. The man disappeared into the shadows and was gone.

At 0410, we heard the choppers coming but didn't see any of them until the first one set down. They were flying with no lights visible from the outside. "Okay, group one, follow me. Don't waste any time," said the lieutenant. They were loaded and gone in less than a minute.

"There comes our ride," said Sergeant Ryan. "Come with me, group two." Group two loaded efficiently, and they were also gone in less than a minute.

Then the sky was quiet for about two minutes. Out of the darkness came our bird. "Here's our 'copter, better late than never. Come on guys," said the gunny. The five of us jumped aboard, and we had a ride out of there. All seventeen of us were safely airborne, and it was only 0416. It had only taken six minutes for three whirlybirds to swoop in, without lights, extract us, and be back in the air flying toward freedom for eight ex-POWs.

Before long, we were flying over the water, and then we swung south. The five of us were chattering like magpies. This was the first time we had been picked up and flown back from one of these missions. The excitement died down after a while, and all of us were soon dozing off. I woke up when we set down back at the landing strip we'd flown out of.

The others got up slowly, and we climbed out. There to meet us was Captain Gordon. He grabbed every one of us and asked, "Do you guys know what you have just done?"

"Well, hell yeah, we were there the whole time," mumbled Gunny.

"What I'm talking about—" said the captain, "you have rescued the first POWs since the truce over three years ago. We were told by the North Koreans that these POWs did not exist!"

Lieutenant Skinner turned to the captain and said, "Captain Gordon, you must be associating with the wrong people then."

We all laughed and he told us, "You're the only people on earth that can get away with talking to me like that. Now, we have to get your team back to Seoul for debriefing, if they are ever gonna let you out in public again. These other eight guys want to talk to you, but they won't be on the same bus with you."

All eight men came over, shook hands, and hugged each and every one of us. We all started crying. Now I know why we do what we do.

That makes it pretty simple. They turned and left us. That was the first time we had seen them cry. It was all real to them now.

Captain Gordon said, "Into the bus everybody. We have to get you back down to Seoul and get you cleaned up for a good meal. Then we will have a full day of debriefing. Doc, are there any injuries to be taken care of on the way?"

I replied, "Grayson has a wound in his leg that needs attention, and I need to see a dentist pretty soon, maybe before I eat." The captain said there was an army hospital just outside Seoul and he would stop there with us while the others went on to the barracks with the rest of the team.

At the hospital, Grayson and I were taken to the emergency room first. The army medic looked into my mouth and swabbed around my teeth with some awful tasting medication. He asked me what happened and Captain Gordon said that I had run into a door. The medic looked at me and raised his eyebrows.

"It was a big door," I said. He then wiggled my teeth to see how loose they were. "There are no teeth broken but seven appear to be loose. I'll have someone get you to the dentist's office and see what he wants to do to them."

I looked at Captain Gordon and said, "I already knew all that, and I don't need to see a dentist now." I just didn't feel comfortable with a dentist I didn't know for some unexplainable reason.

The captain told the medic that I could see a dentist at the next duty station and asked about Grayson who was in the cubicle next to me. The medic over there said that Grayson's wound was clean and that he had put a clean dressing on it; he was ready to go.

Captain Gordon took us out to the front desk and arranged transportation over to the marine barracks. "What are you going to do about your teeth? I could tell you didn't want anything done to them here."

I replied, "He sounded like they wanted to pull them or something. I have a good friend that's a dentist aboard ship and he can take care of them for me."

Then Grayson said, "You did a good job on my leg, Doc. The medic back there said whoever treated me at the last hospital cleaned the wound out really good."

"Thanks Grayson. It was just a scratch," I replied.

We arrived at the barracks and went in with the other men. Gunny said, "We've made arrangements with the chow hall to have a good breakfast ready for you in thirty minutes. You will have time to eat and get back over here to meet with the debriefing officer at 1100 hours. So, get cleaned up, and we'll march over together."

After another good breakfast and plenty of hot coffee, we were all feeling better. I could chew on the right rear teeth if I didn't get into a big hurry. My whole mouth was sore, and the lower lip was swollen badly. It glistened with the Bactine ointment I kept rubbing on it. Good food and hot oatmeal will cure a lot of things.

Back at the barracks, Lieutenant Skinner took us to a meeting room with a large conference table and armchairs. We made ourselves comfortable, but Captain Gordon came in, we popped to our feet. "Good morning, gentlemen. At ease! My name is US Marine Captain Steven Gordon, and I am your debriefing officer today."

Everyone applauded and laughed, but we settled down quickly when he didn't smile. "This session will be handled a little differently than usual. All of you are to be commended for your accomplishments on this mission. You each did an outstanding job. Needless to say this is a very hot topic and could be politically embarrassing to both sides, despite the fact that we brought missing men home. I cannot stress enough how confidential this must remain. Under no circumstances will you relate your participation in this action to anyone. Repeat, DO NOT TELL ANYONE WHAT YOU DID OR WHAT YOU SAW!"

At this point, several officers and noncoms came into the room, and one sat down beside each of us with stacks of paperwork. "You will all be interviewed in this room together. Your statements have been typed out for you. After you've read and understood the statements, you'll sign them in the presence of your respective debriefing officer. Are there any questions? I didn't think there were. Now, read and sign your paperwork."

The marine staff sergeant handed me the three-page statement to read. It said that we were on a four-day training mission practicing rescue and recovery in northern South Korea and on the coastline of the Yellow Sea. We were flying with three helicopters. One of the helicopters had engine trouble on the second day, and we stayed at one location until the engine was repaired, and we were all able to fly back to the airstrip at Munsan together. There was no contact with any hostile troops while on the training mission, and we did not cross the DMZ into North Korea. There was more to the statement than that, but the other two pages of mumbo jumbo were too much to read and talk about.

"That sounds right to me, Sergeant," I said as I signed the statement. "It sure was a boring four days."

"You have a very good memory, Doc," he replied.

Captain Gordon stood up, "Now that all of you have written and signed your statement, go back to the barracks area. We'll all stay here for the next few days. Doc and Kwan, you will both stay here and not go back to your duty stations just yet. You have the rest of the day to get everything squared away. Your equipment and weapons will continue to be locked up for now. Tomorrow morning, the gunny will make them available for cleaning as needed. Report back to this room at 1300 hours tomorrow. Dismissed!"

"Aye, aye, sir!"

Chapter 4

Pyongyang

The sun was shining brightly outside as we walked into the conference room. No one wanted to come inside after coming back from the chow hall. We had been inside the barracks all morning cleaning our weapons, brushing boots with saddle soap for waterproofing, and washing clothes. We were all squared away and wondering why we were still in isolation.

At 1300 hours, Lieutenant Skinner came into the room and called out, "At ease, men," before anyone could call us to attention. "Is everyone caught up on their sleep, and are all of your injuries okay now?" Before we could say anything much, he said, "We all heard the POWs say the other day that there were more men in the Pyongyang area. The army captain said there were twenty-one Americans that he knew of, and we got five of them out, so we've got more work to do if you men are up to it.

"They want us to go after them as soon as possible before they can move the POWs. You have first refusal on this mission. If anyone doesn't feel they ought to go this time, we certainly understand. Do not give me an answer today, but we'll be back in here tomorrow at 0800 hours. For the rest of the afternoon, we'll go over some of the details of the proposed mission, so you'll have an idea of what you might be up against."

Gunny stood up and said, "Pardon me, Lieutenant, I've looked around the room and from the nods I got, we can go ahead with your plans. This team is with you all the way, sir."

Lieutenant Skinner dropped back in his chair, "Are you sure about that, Gunny?" he asked. As a unit, or as a team I should say, we all stood, and Gunny replied, "Here's your answer, sir."

The lieutenant told us to relax and he would be back in a couple minutes and left the room. Gunny said, "Look, men, did I read anybody wrong? Let me know now before he gets back here." Everyone let Gunny know we were in agreement with him. We had to get those guys home.

The lieutenant came back in with Captain Gordon, and they stood in front of us and looked around. "Doc, you and Grayson were wounded earlier this week. Both of you stand up now and tell me whether you can make it or not."

We both stood and Lance Corporal Grayson said, "Doc patched me up, sir, and the doctors have told me I was cleared for duty."

And I said, "I just have a couple loose teeth, but they are not going to fall out. I'm good to go, sir."

"You two have a seat. Neither of you would tell me any different if Jesus Christ was standing here. Take a break and be back here for a long session at 1400 hours."

We went down to the snack room, got a drink, and went outside for a smoke. "I knew we'd get a chance to go back for those other POWs," said Ryan. "I wonder how many men we'll need on this one, probably fourteen or fifteen. But we don't need to talk about it yet."

Corporal Sawkowski told us, "I heard the POWs talking while we were at the camp. They wanted to go back with us to get the others before they left the country."

"That ain't gonna happen," said the gunny. "It's up to us; let's get back in there. Bring your drinks with you."

We got back in our seats, and there were maps, a slide projector, and an overhead projector. This was sure going to be a long day. Lieutenant Skinner and Captain Gordon came in with a Korean gentleman who wore a civilian suit and tie. "At ease, men. Have a seat. This is a South Korean army intelligence officer, and we'll address him as Captain," said Captain Gordon. "We have maps, slides, pictures, and a lot of other information to review this week. First of all, Sergeant Kwan will bring in a replacement for Corporal Park tomorrow. We'll also have three Turkish soldiers with the team who know the area because they were prisoners at Pyongyang for over a year. Two other members of the marine Recon Team will be joining us, so there will be fifteen men on this mission. The timeline hasn't been set, but there will be two to three days of training and preparation before we can do anything."

That afternoon, we saw pictures of the POWs that were taken by Intelligence, pictures of several locations, and overheads of maps showing roads and buildings. There was a lot of studying to do. Captain Gordon stood up, "Our Intelligence talked with the men you brought home this week. They gave us more data than we could have hoped for. We now have street names, buildings, and people's names. Captain here talked with them and knows the area like the back of his hand. Let's go over these maps and pictures one more time today, and we'll start fresh again at 0730 hours tomorrow with the full team."

The next morning, we marched to the chow hall, had breakfast, and marched back for our meeting at 0730. There were cookies, coffee, juice, and soft drinks in the back of the conference room. Then we saw the new faces around the room. The Turkish soldiers were standing off to the side by themselves. There were two USMC privates that I had not seen before, but the other marines all seemed to know them.

Ryan called me over, "Doc, meet Private Holder and Private Harris; Privates, this is Doc Gentry." We all shook hands, and I learned they both had been on two missions before. These were all experienced marines and were probably hand-selected by Gordon and Skinner.

"Attention on deck," came from the front of the room as Captain Gordon, Lieutenant Skinner, and the Korean captain entered. "At ease men. Everyone find a seat. I see you've met the replacements. We're fortunate to have three soldiers from Turkey who'll join us on this mission. They're Sergeant Gulay, Sergeant Berkant, and Sergeant Serhat. You can make personal introductions during next break. As I told you yesterday, they were prisoners of the North Koreans in Pyongyang before they escaped fourteen months ago. They know the area as well as knowing some of the POWs that we'll be looking for."

The next two hours were spent reviewing the maps and pictures with input from the captain and the Turkish soldiers. The POWs were—or were at one time—being held in a small village just south of Pyongyang in shacks that were locked and well guarded at night. The prisoners were being used for working on the railroad, patching roads, and mostly for working the fields on nearby farms owned by the state. "I'd suggest you select a four-man or five-man reconnaissance team to assess the situation before you move the whole team in to effect a rescue," said the captain.

"That's my thought exactly, Captain," said Lieutenant Skinner. "That is our usual procedure in most cases." And that went on for the rest of the day. The Turkish soldiers had substantial input and Captain Gordon, Lieutenant Skinner, and the unnamed Korean captain were very satisfied with the plans at this point.

Captain Gordon called us to order just before we left for dinner at the mess hall. "You men will fall in tomorrow at 0700 in front of the barracks. The gunny will run you through a series of training exercises while we put the final touches on our plan and get the final approvals. You have at least three days training ahead, so get prepared. Dismissed!"

"Aye, aye, sir!"

When we got outside the meeting room, Corporal Reeves asked, "Gunny, we've been talking, instead of going to the chow hall; how about us going to the Slop Chute for a couple hours?" He was referring to the Navy/marine enlisted men's bar and grill that served beer for ten cents a glass and po'boy sandwiches for twenty-five cents. "That way we can all get acquainted with the Turks."

Gunny laughed, "Good thinking, Reeves. I think it's a great idea, but go easy on the brew. You know I'm going to be sweating it out of everyone tomorrow. Okay, you guys, fall in double file. We've got an interesting evening coming up. Forward, march! Left, right, left …"

A good time was had by all at the Slop Chute the previous night. It appeared we had a very cohesive team, at least when it came to eating and drinking. At 0700, all fourteen of us fell in at the barracks, and Gunny started us off with a five-mile jog. "Don't say you weren't warned about today. I told you I'd sweat those beers out of you," he said as we started off. It was a full day of running, exercising, and battling the obstacle course. "Tomorrow, you'll fall out at 0700, and we'll go to the rifle range for four hours to work on a couple things, and then in the afternoon we'll be back into the meeting room. Okay, fall in, and we'll end the day with a short two-mile jog. It's been a full day. Let's get this done. By the way, no Slop Chute tonight."

The following day was spent at the rifle range and in the conference room. Gunny checked us all out on the Garand 03 sniper rifle, BAR, and 1911 .45 cal. pistol. They had a Thompson machine gun that all of us fired fifteen rounds with. I had never fired one before. The Turkish soldiers were all expert riflemen, which wasn't a surprise. Our team members held their own on the range. Back at the meeting room, the captain went over our operational assignments and reviewed the routes we would be taking, showing the maps and locations of the prisoners. "No date has been set as of this morning. We need two more days of preparation before we are ready. We can't take any chances on this one. We'll see you here at 0700 tomorrow. Get a good night's rest."

All the men were getting restless with the training and classroom instructions. They were ready to hit the deck running. We had gotten eight men out of a miserable place, and there were more waiting to get out of there. We had eaten breakfast before 0700 and were in the conference room, sipping coffee and ready to go. Captain Gordon, Lieutenant Skinner, and "Captain" came in early and were surprised to see us all there. "We didn't expect to see the hired hands here before we got set up," said Lieutenant Skinner.

"Tell us what you need done, and this crew will square it away in a heartbeat," said Staff Sergeant Ryan. "This team is ready."

Captain Gordon walked around the room and said, "I think you're ready too. We got the word at 0500 today that you'll gear up and fly out this afternoon. I can tell you now that the 'captain' will be on the ground when you get to your objective. He will be in civilian clothing and will assist Sergeant Kwan and Private Rho to make contact with two other men who will help hide you when you arrive in the village."

The mission got underway before anyone hardly knew what was going on, but that's the way it always happened.

At least we were already in South Korea and didn't have to take the C-47 ride across the Sea of Japan. Back at the barracks, we started packing our gear and checking out our weapons, but Gunny said the ammunition would be issued shortly. The lieutenant had arranged for my medical packs to be delivered to me at the barracks. All the medical supplies that I would need seemed correct, and I had already made sure that each team member had their individual first-aid kits stocked and on their belts.

"Okay, men, get your gear together," said Gunny. "Grab your weapons and load up. It's time to pick up our ammunition, grenades, and Ryan's hardware. Fall in at the curb double file."

We grabbed our gear and looked around, making sure we hadn't left anything behind. In about ten minutes, we were in step with the gunny and on our way. We loaded up on the ammo and our hardware, marched to Operations, and climbed on the two trucks waiting for us.

"Where's our bus? Lance Corporal Edwards asked.

"You're in the marine Corps again; this ain't the air force!" replied Gunny. We were on the way north to the landing strip and the helicopter base near Munsan.

As usual, it was quiet after we got on the road. Everyone was thinking about the upcoming mission into North Korea to search for the American prisoners. It was exciting to be involved in such an important mission. The trucks pulled through the gate at the Munsan helicopter base and parked by the tents. "Off the trucks and fall in by the tent," Gunny said. "We'll stand by here until the lieutenant confirms our orders and the departure time is set. Fall out by the fence, and we'll wait and see what the scoop is."

"There you are again, Gentry" I heard someone say. I turned around and there was Hospital Corpsman Third Class Young, my buddy from hospital corps school, "Are you here on R & R again?"

I shook hands with him saying, "Yeah, we're all on vacation. Let me introduce you to someone." We walked over to Gunny, who was watching us closely. "Gunny, this is Corpsman Young, he and I went to school at Great Lakes. Lanny, meet Gunnery Sergeant Potter, the brains behind this outfit."

Gunny replied, "I've met Young before. He has taken care of our medical supplies for over a year. How you doing, Doc? By the way, you know you didn't see any of this."

Young laughed as he added, "I'm doing good, Gunny. I haven't seen any of you coming through here for a year or more."

We talked for a while and Lanny checked to see if there was anything else we needed. Lieutenant Skinner came back and called us together. "We'll hold here and board the 'copters at 2130. We'll take three helicopters this time and depart at 2200 hours. Sergeant Ryan, go over to the operations tent and arrange for a good dinner for us at the chow hall. We have time for a good hot meal." That suited all of us, for sure. "Corpsman Young, what are you doing here? I've not see you up here with the working men before," said the lieutenant, slapping Lanny on the back.

"Hi Lieutenant Skinner, I just got back from a day at my private beach and wanted to see how the lower class was living" joked Young. "You're about to take an unscheduled flight on a helicopter to nowhere talking like that," laughed Skinner.

"I was just leaving," he replied. "You guys have a good trip. I have to get back to work." We shook hands and he jumped into his jeep and headed back to his medical aid station.

We stowed our gear and weapons in a tent next to Operations. After a good meal at the chow hall, we were led over to the tent with our gear near the helicopters where we could relax for an hour or so. The pads on the cots were thin but comfortable at times like this. We slept for over an hour, and Staff Sergeant Ryan came in at 2100 hours. "That's as long as you ground-pounders can goof off. Hit the deck. We board the birds in thirty minutes. Take care of business and get your gear on. Fall out in five minutes."

Lieutenant Skinner stood in front of our formation. "Check each others' buckles and packs so we don't lose anything or anyone. We'll board three helicopters in teams of five. I'm in the first helicopter with Corporal Ski, Corporal Grayson, Sergeant Kwan, and Doc. Gunny Potter, you're in the second one with Corporal Reeves, Private Holder, Private Harris, and Private Rho. And then, Staff Sergeant Ryan, you go in the third bird with Corporal Edwards, Sergeants Gulay, Berkant, and Serhat. Fall in with your team, and let's get going."

By the time we climbed aboard our helicopter and stowed the gear for the flight, it was time to lift off. Everyone noticed, but no one said anything about the helicopters being painted with North Korean markings. And away we go ... but no Jackie Gleason here!

Within forty-five minutes, we were out over the Yellow Sea and turned north. "I can tell you guys what I told the gunny and Sergeant Ryan—we couldn't fly directly north from the airstrip across the DMZ. After we fly up over the sea for thirty minutes, we'll turn inland and take a direct route toward Pyongyang. We'll fly over Sariwon, where we were last trip, and to a spot just south of Pyongyang and east of Kangnam near the railroad. That's where we'll meet the captain and his people. The helicopters have oversized fuel tanks, and the captain has made arrangements to have additional fuel if it is needed. This is a three-hour flight, so now you know what comes next."

We approached our objective at 0135 hours; the helicopters slowed and stayed about six hundred yards apart to make it easier to drop each team and move out for the next. The terrain was rocky, and the boulders prevented the helicopters from landing. We came in first at about twenty feet and rappelled out on the signal as the 'copter kept moving, slowly stringing us out on the GO. The second team came in the same way and moved out. The third helicopter came in low and set one skid on the side of the hill, while the team jumped out and then unloaded Sergeant Ryan's *hardware*. As each team landed, we ran about forty yards into the trees bordering the clearing. Then the helicopters flew off into the night for their return trip. The gunny and I checked with each man to make sure there were no injuries.

"Give me a count, Gunny," said the lieutenant. "We have to get moving before we have company again. We're three or four miles from our rendezvous point with the captain and his men. They'll be expecting us no later than 0300."

"We have all fifteen accounted for and ready to go, Lieutenant. Let's move out, men. Sergeant Kwan will lead the patrol at point with Holder, and Harris bringing up the rear. Keep it quiet and be sharp," Gunny said.

The moon was fairly bright and the weather was just warm enough to knock the chill off the night air. Walking up and down the mountainous trails kept us warm enough. At 0240, Sergeant Kwan held up his hand and then motioned us to get down on the ground. "Lieutenant, we are close to the place to meet the captain. I need to scout ahead to confirm our location and contact the captain."

"Okay, Sergeant, take Rho, Holder, and Harris with you. Use the one-two-three signal when you return."

Kwan replied, "Will do, sir. Come on you three and keep it quiet." They moved on up the trail and were out of sight in less than a minute.

The rest of us settled by the trees and boulders and kept our eyes and ears open for anything that might turn up. So far, there had been no sign of life, except for an occasional light from a house in the distance when we walked over a ridge.

Suddenly, there was a single flash of light up ahead, and then in ten seconds, there were two more flashes. The gunny flashed a light in return after another ten seconds. Several shadowy figures appeared on the trail coming toward us. Sergeant Kwan approached, and then we all stood up from our places of concealment. The captain walked toward the lieutenant, and they shook hands.

The captain and his men were dressed as farmers so they would not draw undue attention to the small group. "Welcome to my former home," said the captain. "I have five men who grew up here and are anxious to help find your missing soldiers."

Lieutenant Skinner replied, "Thank your men for us, Captain.

We're glad to have your help. It's now 0330; how far can we go before daylight?"

"There is a place two hours from here that will be about two miles from our first objective, and it will be a secure location for you to spend most of the day. While you are resting, my team and I will be visiting the area the Americans were last seen by our operatives."

The captain and Lieutenant Skinner moved out of our hearing and talked for another six or eight minutes. Then the lieutenant got us to our feet, "Up and at 'em, men. Two more hours and you can take a break. Move out. The captain's men will take point, and everyone needs to be alert. No unnecessary talking from here on."

As we advanced, we were coming down out of the mountainous region. There were still trees and wooded areas. Thank goodness, there were not as many rocks, and the walking was much easier. There were twenty-one in our group now, and they were strung out for a good distance in four- to five-foot intervals. At 0540, the Koreans led us over to a clump of trees, and there was a cave, which we entered. Each of us snapped on our flashlights. The opening was about three feet wide and five feet high. Six feet into the mouth, the tunnel made a ninety degree left turn, and then after four or five feet, there was a ninety-degree turn to the right. Then we walked into a room easily twenty by twenty feet square. "There's another room through this opening," said one of the Koreans as he shined his light to the rear, "you will find sleeping bags and a supply of food and water for us all. There is also a back door through that room."

To everyone's amazement, he spoke in perfect English. Then he asked, "Do any of you know where Wake Forest College is?"

I replied, "Yes, it's now in Winston-Salem, North Carolina, which is thirty-five miles from where I was raised." He laughed, saying, "I enjoy fooling everyone with my English. I got my undergraduate degree and my doctorate at the Baptist seminary in Wake Forest, North Carolina, in 1948—all before they moved to Winston-Salem. I also played baseball at the college. Just call me Joe Smith." Everyone got a big laugh, and then he said, "Call me Chaplain Huang. That's how I first got into this outfit. But, don't let that part fool you; I still carry a rifle and pistol. It's still a way of life here—just like your pioneers."

"Enough of that," said Gunny, "We've gotta settle down and get some rest so we can get our job done."

The captain told the lieutenant that we would not have to set a guard, but Lieutenant Skinner said, "In all respect, sir, we will still post a guard at each opening. That's how we operate. Sergeant Ryan will set the schedule. I understand your men will take a two-hour break here before you leave."

Sergeant Gulay spoke up, "If you don't mind, Lieutenant, my men would like to take first watch duty. We've been inactive for two weeks and want to take part in all duties."

"That will be fine, Sergeant. You have the first three hours, and Sergeant Ryan will set a rotation schedule from there. Everyone find your spot and settle down. Get something to eat and get some rest." It had really been an easy night, but we could always eat and sleep.

I stood up, and Corporal Sawkowski said, "We know, Doc: 'Take off your boots and socks, use the powder, and put on dry socks.' We know the drill."

Then Corporal Reeves spoke up, "Yeah, put a sock in it, Doc."

When the laughter died down, I said, "Well, it looks like I got the message across to you Jarheads: take care of your feet, because we are not going to carry you out of here piggy back." About a dozen boots came flying toward me. We were getting silly now, so it was time to get some rest.

Just after 0800, the captain and his men left out on their patrol. "Take care of everyone Chaplain Joe Smith," I called out.

"Bless you, my son" he replied.

Then they were out and gone. It was time to get some more sleep, but most of us were already feeling like we should do something. After a couple hours lying around, I went through some of my gear, checked over my weapons, and then sharpened my bayonet. One of the Turkish soldiers was sharpening what looked like a crooked dagger and then put it back in the sheath. "What kind of knife is that, Sergeant?" I asked him, I still didn't know one of them from the other. He told me what kind of dagger it was, but I didn't understand the name. "Could I see it?" I asked.

"Of course you may, my friend," as he drew the dagger from his sheath and then slowly pulled the blade across his forearm until a small trickle of blood beaded up. He then wiped the blade on his pant leg and handed me the dagger—handle first.

I hesitantly took it and asked, "Why did you do that?"

To which he replied, "We swore an oath that each time we pull our knife we will draw blood, and I do not draw the blood of my friends!"

The Untold Experiences of a Navy Corpsman

I looked at the knife quickly, felt the razor-sharp blade, and handed it back to him—handle first. "Thank you," was all I could think to say. Then all three of the Turks burst out laughing, probably at the look on my face.

The captain and his team returned around 1300 hours. The lieutenant, Gunny, and Sergeant Ryan went outside with the captain. They were in deep conversation for nearly an hour, going over maps; Ryan was taking notes. I was on guard duty at the entrance and could hear very little they were saying. The number sixteen came up three or four times, but I could not understand in what context. I just kept my mouth shut and listened. That has always been pretty good advice.

Lieutenant Skinner called us outside and into a circle, and the captain posted his men on guard. "First things first," said the lieutenant. "The captain is certain there are sixteen men imprisoned in a small compound near the railroad. At least eleven of them are Americans, and the others may be Australians. Second, at least three North Korean patrols were seen in the area today. At 1730, we'll move out to the objective and implement our plan to rescue those prisoners.

"There are twenty-one of us, and according to the captain's surveillance today, there are approximately fifty North Korean soldiers in the compound. There's no fencing around the ten buildings, but there are guard towers on the top of two buildings on opposite sides of the small base. They appear to have two barracks and one chow hall for the soldiers. The prisoners are housed in one building and probably have their food brought to them. That's the usual procedure according to the captain's men who were once prisoners in this area."

The lieutenant asked for questions and then said, "You'll divide into the same teams that we assigned on the helicopter flight. The captain and his men will be the fourth team. Now, fall out with your team, and you will be briefed on your assignments."

Lieutenant Skinner called our team together: Corporal Sawkowski, Lance Corporal Grayson, Sergeant Kwan, and me. "After the other teams are in place, each of you stay with me as we approach the building the prisoners are housed in. Here it is on the map, and the guards' barracks are on the opposite side of the yard. We'll have to go around a supply building to get to them. We'll try to get them out without a firefight, but the other teams will have that part covered while we're concentrating on the prisoners."

Just then, Gunny came over and told everyone to get their weapons and stay behind the trees. "A North Korean patrol's coming up the path close to us. I counted twelve soldiers with their weapons slung, so they're not looking for us. Just stay quiet, because we don't want to jeopardize our mission tonight."

The patrol moved on by but stopped for a short break before they were out of sight. They moved on toward the railroad after about five minutes.

"We know they're out there now," said Lieutenant Skinner. "Get your gear ready. We move out in ten minutes—that'll be 1735 hours—and we'll take a little different route from the patrol that just passed by. Okay. Be safe, be sharp, and be tough."

We gathered our gear and weapons preparing for this next adventure. For the next couple minutes, I kneeled in prayer, and when I stood up and turned around, I saw I was not the only one.

We assembled outside the cave, and the captain and his men disguised the entrance to our cave with brush. "Fall in with your team and move out," said Gunny. The captain and his team took point, and each team followed them. It was not quite dark yet, but we needed to get close enough to see where the guards were locating themselves and to get an idea where the rest of them were going. The walking was easy here—the foothills were low, and there were enough trees to help conceal our movements.

It took over thirty minutes to reach the point where we could observe our objective. The gunny spread us out so we could all see but not *be* seen. The captain and Lieutenant Skinner trained their binoculars on the compound. Sergeant Ryan pointed over to our right where a twelve-man patrol was moving in toward the compound. It looked like the same patrol we had seen earlier by our cave. We heard a train coming up the valley and then saw the railroad about seventy-five yards on the other side of the compound. Twenty minutes later, a group of men walked into our view, followed by armed guards. "I count eighteen men in line and six guards," said Lieutenant Skinner.

"I get the same count, Lieutenant Skinner," answered the captain. The men walked straight to the building that was marked on our map as the POW's quarters.

"So far, so good. It's starting to get dark enough to make our move," said the lieutenant, "but we have to give them time to get settled in before we stir up the hornet's nest."

We watched their movements for another hour, and the Koreans had gone in and out of the chow hall and now seemed to be settling down in the barracks. Then, four soldiers came out of the chow hall carrying boxes and made their way to the POW's building. One of them set his box down and took down the bar and opened the door. They put the boxes inside the hut and closed the door. The four men then went back to the chow hall, turned out the lights, and entered the first barracks.

"The bar seems to be the only way to secure the door. It looks like a five-foot two-by-four and it may have pegs in each end. They didn't use a key in the lock," said the lieutenant. "There appear to be two small windows no more than eight inches square on this side of the building. They won't be of any help. There aren't any guards visible in the two guard huts on top of the buildings." There wasn't any movement visible from our vantage point. "Let's wait until 2200 hours and see if there is any more activity. How does that sound, Captain?"

"That sounds good, Lieutenant. They're not expecting us tonight."

The only activity since the POWs were fed involved a guard making one tour around the compound every twenty minutes—like clockwork. He was always by himself and did not carry a rifle on his rounds. "They definitely don't expect anything tonight, but it won't make it that much easier. Let's be sure we're not the ones that get surprised," said Gunny. "Are we still on for 2200 hours, Lieutenant?"

"Most definitely, Gunny. Get everyone ready and we'll move into position."

We all took a good drink of water, and most of us ate a little snack. I always kept a couple chocolate bars in my jacket pocket, as did most everyone else.

"One last briefing before we move out. When you get into position, as you know, make sure you won't fire on each other in case we have to take action. That'll probably happen, so be careful of each other. Edwards, Grayson, and Holder have grenade launchers, which will be fired at first sign of trouble. That's one on each of the marine teams. When you get the order to fire, pick your targets. I'm for getting those guys out of here and back safely to their loved ones. It is now 2140; we have twenty minutes to get ready to move. Get with your team."

Just as we started to move down the hill to our assigned locations, the lights in the two small buildings in front of the barracks went out, and two men from each building walked over to the second barracks. "I hope they leave the lights on inside the barracks for another thirty minutes. They can't see out the windows as long as they leave them on. Hold up for a few minutes; it's time for the guard to make his rounds, and he hasn't come out yet."

We waited another ten minutes, and then we saw the guard. He must have changed his rounds to every thirty minutes after 2200. He walked by the POW's building, checking the bar on the door, and soon made it back to the barracks. He went into the first barracks by the chow hall. It was now 2225, so we started down the hill the second time toward our positions.

Lieutenant Skinner held us into position until the guard made his rounds again. At 2300 hours, he came out and started his tour of the compound. He made one walk around the entire compound and returned to his barracks. "Okay, we're making our move now. Corporal Sawkowski, lead the way. Let's go. Look sharp, guys."

We followed Ski on in across the access road, around the supply hut, and up to the prisoners' building. Kwan moved around the building and back to us. It was too quiet. Kwan and Ski went to the door, removed the pegs from each end and then the bar. Ski reached over and opened the door and shined a flashlight into a group of startled eyes. Lieutenant Skinner went to the door, shined in his light, and said, "Keep quiet. I am Lieutenant Skinner of the US Marines. Who are you, and who is in charge?"

"My God, Lieutenant, we are Americans and have been here for years! How did you find us?" answered a voice with a strong Southern accent.

"We'll talk later, gentlemen; all of you follow us out of here. We have a little help outside, so keep it quiet and come on." It was unbelievable as they filed out and we led them up the hill. All of a sudden, spotlights blazed alive, and the whole compound was as bright as day. Our men opened up with the grenades. Grayson was with us, so he turned around and fired one grenade toward each barracks. Then everyone opened up on the soldiers running out of the barracks. There was very little fire coming from the compound. Someone was shooting out the lights, and the lieutenant, Gunny, Ski, and I kept herding the prisoners up and over the hill. We looked back, and most of the lights were out; our men were still shooting and lobbing grenades into the compound. All of a sudden, a huge explosion occurred in the center of the yard where the vehicle shed was located, and most all the buildings burst into flame. Looks like Ryan was busy while we were getting the prisoners out.

"Gunny, you, and Ski go back and help with the cleanup. Doc and I will stay here with our guests."

"Aye, aye, sir, Come on, Ski."

We turned around to the unbelieving ex-prisoners and asked how many there were and if they had any injuries. "I am US Army Captain John Winters. I haven't said that in a long time. There are eighteen of us at this location. Eleven of us are American—nine Army and two marines. We have five Australian soldiers who were in our company, and there are two South Korean army, who have been here only two or three weeks. As far as I know, we have no new injuries, but several have ailments from old injuries and lack of medical care."

The lieutenant told them to sit tight; as soon as we had our men together, we'd move out to our camp for a couple hours until we could get all our gear and move out of the area.

"Lieutenant, I'd better go down and see if there are any injuries. There doesn't seem to be much more going on," I said.

"Maybe that'd be a good idea, Doc. Be careful," replied Lieutenant Skinner.

I slowly walked down the hill with my carbine at ready. The moon was coming out pretty bright by now. I saw Gunny and went over to him. "What's the report on injuries, Gunny?"

"None so far, Doc. We have accounted for everyone, and if anyone's hurt, they haven't realized it yet." He called the teams together and got them headed up the hill to join the others.

"The only sounds we are hearing are from ammo exploding in the fires," said Sergeant Ryan. "I was able to set charges under three buildings before all hell broke loose. Let's get everyone out before someone else shows up."

Lieutenant Skinner called us together. "We'll be moving up to our base camp in the cave and get out of sight while we get organized. Captain, lead us out. Gunny, get a count as we move out."

"Aye aye, sir. Doc, bring up the rear and help me with the count." I moved around with Gunny and we both came up with the same count. "Thirty-three souls counted, Lieutenant, and we're on the move."

We arrived at the cave and got everyone inside without further incident. "Gunny,, put six men outside on guard. Keep the perimeter close in and well concealed."

Gunny replied, "They're already in position, Lieutenant." It was crowded in the large cavern, but a lot of laughing, handshaking, and hugging was going on.

The captain shouted out to us, "These two are my men that I told you were lost three weeks ago! They were captured near the railroad on one of our surveillance trips." So now, the captain had seven men on his team.

Lieutenant Skinner then got with the army captain and an Australian sergeant over to the side and asked them about other POWs. "There are many others, but none of them are near here that I know of. At one time, probably six months ago, there were forty-five prisoners here, mostly American—army, marines, and airmen. They're all moved all about the country from time to time. They didn't keep us in any one place long at a time," said the army captain.

The captain broke in and said now would be a good time to put some distance between us and the prison compound. "This area will be flooded with soldiers before noon, looking for us. We have weapons in the other room to arm most of these men. There is another place we can get to about six miles southwest of here where we can make contact with your helicopter base."

I was making rounds of all the POWs and our men, making sure there were no injuries before we left. Several of the POWs had wounds and sores that needed attention. I cleaned, medicated, and bandaged them as needed. It took well over an hour. That would hold them until we got to a better facility. Ski and Reeves had received cuts in the skirmish, which I took care of as well. I then turned my attention to Ryan, who had a severe burn on his left hand and forearm. I covered it with Furacin gauze and bandaged it good. At least there were no bullet wounds—amazing!

Gunny said we had caught the North Koreans completely by surprise and had been well deployed and ready for their defensive fight. "I am sure some of them were able to escape our attack but probably not many. It appears they'd become complacent and thought they had the POWs secured and would not be raided. Let that be a lesson everybody. Always be prepared."

Lieutenant Skinner called out, "Hold it down. Get all your gear together. The captain has a few rifles, ammo, and supplies for our guests in case we need their help. We are going to get out of here and move to a place away from this area. The captain will be able to contact our base and get everyone out. Let's move out. You had better fix bayonets for the rest of this trip. The captain's men are at point. Our new friends are next, and we'll bring up the rear. Be safe, be alert, and be sharp."

It was a little uncomfortable moving thirty-three men in hostile territory. We couldn't hear vehicle noises, but it seemed there were eyes behind every tree. The captain was leading us at a good, steady pace. I'm glad they knew where they were going. We were in the lowlands with trees and underbrush that concealed us fairly well. The sky was getting lighter by the minute, but we kept moving.

Just after 0600, as we were following the edge of the tree line, we began taking fire from off to the left. "Hit the deck! Find a target and return fire. Ryan—take your team back left and flank them—GO, GO, GO!" Sergeant Ryan, Corporal Edwards, and the three Turkish sergeants slipped out through the underbrush.

We were firing selectively for the most part at gun flashes less than a hundred yards away. "Corpsman—Corpsman!" I heard from off to the right. I ran over to Holder, who was calling me and pulled him over behind a couple trees. He had been shot in the left leg and left arm. I cut open the pants and applied a tourniquet around his upper leg. I could tell the bullet was still in his thigh. I then pressed a bandage on his leg and asked him to hold it tightly while I checked his arm. The bullet wound on his arm was like a long cut—a deep graze wound. I wiped the blood off and then tied a compress bandage around his arm. I gave him a shot of morphine and removed the bandage from his thigh. Holding a flashlight in my left hand, I could see the bullet had not penetrated very deeply. I got my forceps on the bullet and slowly removed it. I packed medicated gauze into the wound to stop the bleeding and tied a compress bandage around his thigh. I propped him up against a tree and told him to stay put. I went back around to check on the other guys.

Then we heard Ryan's team open up with their Garands—a very distinctive sound. We held our fire, and very soon, everything was quiet. Ryan and his men soon came into view. "That threat was taken care of," said Ryan. "The Turkish sergeants checked each of them to be sure. There were eight North Korean soldiers in that patrol.

We offered to fashion a stretcher for Holder, but he declined. Corporal Reeves came over with a six-foot long stick to help him hobble along. Lieutenant Skinner told Gunny, Ryan, and the captain to get their respective teams together and get moving again. "It's now 0720, and we've got to get out of here. We're just twenty minutes from our next stop. Move out!"

About a hundred yards down the trail, we heard yelling and gunfire from our right flank. "Here they come again. Take cover; return fire."

We started firing, and twenty or thirty North Koreans were running right at us. I know I hit four of them, because they were that close. Then we realized there were more than twenty or thirty. They just kept coming out of the trees. There were at least fifty of them. Everyone was firing at them and shouting orders. Then we were in hand-to-hand combat—not my first. If I couldn't get a shot at them, I was swinging the butt of my carbine or thrusting with the bayonet. Most of the hostiles did not have bayonets on their rifles, so that was one advantage we had. Some of them did not fire a shot; they just ran toward us yelling. I did pull my .45 and used it until I had a chance to reload the carbine.

Seemingly out of nowhere, mortar shells were falling all around us and more North Koreans were coming out of the woods. KA-BOOM! That's all I remember about this fight.

The following account of the rest of this mission was related to me by Gunnery Sergeant Potter a month later, when he visited me at a hospital in Japan.

Most of the mortar shells fell short of us, except for the three or four that fell among our team. Our recon team, the South Koreans, the POWs, and the North Korean mortar shells killed most of the North Koreans. The official count was forty-one North Koreans. We captured eight including two officers. The captain interrogated them with the aid of Sergeant Berkant—who, I was told, had a way of persuading them to talk.

The captain determined that there were two more patrols searching for us, and they were expecting helicopters to join the search. The North Korean officers finally confirmed that there were many more prisoners being held in Pyongyang and other places in North Korea. The prisoners were turned over to Sergeant Berkant and his two friends, who escorted them back into the woods. I'm sure they turned them loose there!

Sergeant Serhat and Gunny found me and thought I was gone, but then found a pulse. They stopped the bleeding and bandaged the wounds on my back, shoulders, and back of my head. Then they prepared a stretcher for me. Sergeant Sawkowski and Private Harris were not as fortunate. Both of them died of their wounds within a half hour. Corporal Reeves was shot in the chest, and Sergeant Berkant in the shoulder, but both survived. Private Rho and two of the captain's men had medical training and, along with the help of others, treated the wounded. They made more stretchers to carry out the wounded, as well as for Ski and Harris.

The captain led us on to the secure cave. There were three rooms in this cave that meant space for us all. Fifty yards from the cave was a small house that the captain and his men were living in as farmers. On a small hill above our cave was a hidden radio hut. They would use the radio to contact our helicopter base and arrange for transportation for the POWs. There were sleeping bags and blankets piled in the corner of the first large room. In the second room, there was a fireplace built into the wall with a chimney fashioned up and out of the cave. The third room had food, more blankets and sleeping bags, weapons, ammunition, and other supplies. Most everything were U S-issued military supplies.

Lieutenant Skinner stood up on a box and whistled to get everyone's attention, "Okay, down to business, people. We are in a situation here that will require all of us to do our job, whatever it is. The captain's team is manning the radio, contacting our base to get some transportation in here for us. We do not know yet where it will be, nor do we know when it will be. It is over 200 miles back to the DMZ, and we must avoid crossing directly over that. The plans call for helicopters to ferry the *ex-POWs* out first. Depending on circumstances, the captain will lead us southwest toward the sea to be picked up either by helicopter or smuggled out by boat."

That *depending on circumstances* part did not sound just right, according to what the gunny later told me. Then he stood up and said, "Lieutenant, how long will it be before we get word back from the base? We can't stay holed up here for long."

Lieutenant Skinner replied, "We should learn the first part any time now. The first priority is to get the POWs out safely. Then we'll make our way out of here and back to those little tents at the air base. Every one of you get some food and sleep while the plan is put in place to get our guests to their 'copter ride tonight. Gunny, you and Sergeant Ryan set the watch assignments. Unless you hear differently, have all the teams ready to go at 1600. Now, like I said, get some food and sleep. You're going to need it."

No word came in until 1630 hours. The captain sent Chaplain Huang in with the news that "four helicopters will arrive in a clearing two miles west of here at 2200 hours. The POWs, the wounded, and the two dead marines will be picked up and flown back south. Then we'll all march toward the sea and contact the base when we reach our contact in Songnim, which is just twenty miles southeast of here."

"Hey, look at Doc. He's sitting up," Grayson shouted. "Doc, how are you feeling?" I just sat there looking around and lay back down, according to Gunny. About five minutes later, I stood up and started walking around. Everyone talked to me, but I did not reply to anyone. Sergeant Ryan handed me a plate of food, I took it and just stood there looking at it. Ryan took me by the arm, took the plate from my hand, led me over to the wall of the cave, and left me standing there. Apparently, I stood there for five minutes before Ryan again took me by the arm and sat me down. When we left the cave, Ryan tied a four-foot length of rope to my belt, and the rescued POWs led me to the helicopter that night for the flight back south.

The rest of the Marine Recon Team and the South Korean soldiers made it to a bay southwest of Songnim two days later where they were smuggled out in a large fishing boat. Of course, the fishing boat was manned by more of the captain's men.

I have absolutely no memory of this episode after the mortar shell exploded. My memory of the skirmish before the mortar explosion returned while I was lying in a bed in a navy hospital in Japan.

CHAPTER 5

REST AND RELAXATION

Next thing I knew I was in the middle of a hospital ward in pajamas looking up at an IV bottle attached to my arm, and there were leather straps on my arms and legs. My back and head were aching like crazy. "Where am I, and how did I get here?" I asked the guy sitting beside me in a chair between the two beds.

"You're in the US Naval Hospital in Yokosuka, Japan, but I don't know how you got here. You've been in that bed two days and keep saying, 'Look out, here come some more!' or 'I'll get him and you get the other one!' Were you in a bar fight or something?" he asked.

I replied, "Yeah, something like that."

"Hey, Corpsman, you have a live one over here," he called out. A navy corpsman and a navy nurse came over to my bed. "Good morning, marine," she said. "Have you had a good nap?"

"I don't remember much about a nap or anything else." I replied. "How long have I been here and are we really in Yokosuka?"

"You have been here two days, and yes, this is Yokosuka Naval Hospital. You were brought in from Korea night before last. I was on duty when you were admitted, and you were in surgery for over an hour," said the nurse. "We need to remove the restraints so we can dress your wounds and maybe remove the IVs. You will have to stay in bed for now—do you understand that?"

"Sure, I will stay in the bed. Have I been causing problems? By the way, I am not a marine. I'm a Navy Corpsman," I replied.

"You're a corpsman? You came in wearing combat gear," said the corpsman.

"Yes, I'm a corpsman on TDY[1] with the marines, and for the record, I ran into a doorknob."

Everyone laughed, and the nurse said, "That doorknob sure does get around, and it does a lot of damage. Now, turn over on your stomach, and we will dress your doorknob wounds."

The corpsman removed the IV and the restraints while we were talking. The nurse started removing the bandages, cleaning and dressing the wounds. "If I didn't know better, I'd say you were hit by grenade or mortar shrapnel."

"The door knob must have exploded," I said.

"You're sticking to you story, aren't you? That was no damned doorknob. You've been with the marines so long you're beginning to sound like one," replied the nurse.

After they got me all set, they brought in some crackers and a Coke. That sure did taste good. I sat up to eat but had to lie down after a couple minutes, until the room stopped spinning. After an hour or so, two corpsmen came over and sat me up on the side of the bed for a few minutes; then they got me up on my feet. My head was pounding with pain. I was dizzy and unsteady on my feet, but they held on to me. I walked about twenty feet with their help and returned to my bed. They told me to lie back down, and we would do more in an hour.

The corpsmen took me on a couple more short walks, and I ate some cheese crackers and drank some Coke. I was doing much better on my feet, but couldn't walk straight toward anything. I kept veering from left to right, and my balance was still shaky, at best.

While I was eating dinner that evening—my first full meal—I was talking to the marine in the next bed and realized I was slurring my speech bad when I had to repeat several words to him. This was the first time I had noticed anything like that. Everything was still hazy, and I was half-nauseous ever since I'd woken up this morning. I ate about half the food on my tray and had to lie down. The room was starting to spin again.

Two navy doctors came to my bed and checked my reflexes, looked in my eyes, and had me walk back and forth. Then they looked at the wounds on the back of my head and my shoulders. While we were discussing my problem of walking straight, they noticed how I slurred

---

1 Temporary duty.

my speech. One doctor asked me, "Did you have any speech impediment or mobility problems before this injury?"

"No, sir" I replied. "I didn't have any problems at all."

"We need to know how this injury occurred, and don't give us the doorknob story. We heard about that one," said the doctor.

"Sir, may we move to a room where we can talk privately?" I asked him.

"Yes, we need to go to a treatment room anyway. Can you walk to the end of the ward to one of the rooms?"

"No sir, I don't think I can. I'm still weak and very dizzy." He called for a corpsman to bring a wheelchair and move me to a treatment room. When we went into the treatment room, the doctors sent the corpsman out and turned back to me. "I was with a Marine Recon Team in North Korea, and my last memory was being in hand-to-hand combat, and mortar shells were starting to come in on us. Most of them were falling short in the midst of the North Korean soldiers. I don't remember exactly what happened to me until I woke up in the ward earlier. I just know my head hurts terribly, and my back is sore all over."

"Well, Corpsman," replied one of the doctors. "We operated on you when you came in, and we both knew right away you had been hit by mortar shrapnel. It's different from grenade shrapnel in that it is a little heavier. You were very fortunate because it appears you got more of the concussion and less of the flying metal. We don't know all of your symptoms yet, but we do know you have months of therapy ahead of you. You probably won't go back to duty for a year or more."

"Thank you, sir," I said, "but I have to get back sooner than that. There are more POWs up there that we have to get back to their homes and family. One thing: I'm not supposed to be telling you any of this, so if you tell anything I've said, I'll have to kill you both," I said with a smile.

"We're not going to worry about you getting to us in the condition you're in. Just to let you know, that's exactly what Captain Gordon told us you would say," they laughed as they left the room. "Go to bed and get some sleep, Corpsman!"

In the following two weeks, I went through more tests, examinations, x-rays, and blood tests than I can list. I slowly regained my strength, but my balance and speech problems didn't improve very quickly. At least, I was now slowly walking everywhere I went. I bumped into several people as if I were intoxicated, but still got where I wanted to go.

About three weeks into my stay in the hospital, I was eating in the chow hall, when a marine set his tray down across from me, and I heard a familiar voice say, "Doc, what are you doing hanging out in a dump like this?" I looked up and Corporal Ed Reeves was holding his left hand out to me. His right arm was in a sling.

"Reeves! You're the last person in the world I expected to see here. What are you doing here? Have a seat," I said.

"I was shot in the chest in that skirmish on our last trip. Did you get wounded too?"

"Yes," I replied. "But I don't remember anything about it. They say I was hit by one of those mortar rounds. As you can tell, it is affecting my talking, and I can't walk straight either. Do you know if anyone else got hit?"

"No, Doc," he said. "I don't remember anything about it. I didn't even know you were here either." We talked for an hour while we ate and then walked back to the ward. It turned out that we were both in the same ward, just on opposite sides of the room. It was good to see an old friend. He was getting along really well and would be going back to his unit in two weeks.

My doctor came in a few days later and said, "Corpsman, you're going to be sent back to the states to the hospital in Oakland for your speech and mobility therapy. You'll be getting your orders in a day or so."

I went down to the administrative office and checked in with one of the corpsmen that I knew from Camp LeJeune. I asked him to check the itinerary of my ship, the *Anderson* and, if they would be in Yokohama soon, for him to get me on it to get back to Oakland. Long story short, I got my orders the next morning to go to Yokohama and, in three days, to board the *Anderson*. He had worked it so I would go back to San Francisco on the ship and be transferred to Oakland Naval Hospital upon arrival there.

That afternoon, Captain Gordon, Gunnery Sergeant Potter, and Staff Sergeant Ryan walked into the ward, and the nurse brought them back to my bed.

"Now here comes trouble," I said as they approached. "What are you VIPs doing here with the working class?" All the guys around me looked at me as if I were crazy talking to them like that.

All three came over and shook my hand. "How ya' doing, Doc?" asked Captain Gordon.

"You don't look any better, Doc," said Gunny.

"Maybe they can graft on a new head for you while you're here," quipped Sergeant Ryan.

"Okay, you clowns," I replied, "none of you have room to talk."

"The corpsman is going to take us back up front to a room where we can talk. There are a couple things to go over," said Captain Gordon. They put me in a wheelchair and pushed me up the hall to a small conference room.

Inside the room were Corporal Reeves, Private Jackson, and the Turk, Sergeant Berkant, each in their hospital pajamas and robes. "Surprise," said Gunny, "none of you knew the others were here. All of you were wounded in that last skirmish." We shook hands and talked a few minutes. Ed Reeves was the only one I knew had been wounded.

"Hold it down, fellows," said Captain Gordon, "I have some rough news to tell you. You probably don't know that we lost two men in that skirmish. Corporal Sawkowski and Private Harris were wounded and died before we could get them out. There was nothing that could have saved them. All of the POWs made it through.

"Now, after all we've been through together, Lieutenant Skinner was on the way to see his family in Tokyo, and his taxi was hit in the side when a truck ran a stoplight. The lieutenant and the driver were both killed instantly. I don't think he even knew what hit him."

There was stone-cold silence in the room as everyone looked at each other, and then we dropped our heads in disbelief. News of three brothers lost at one time is hard to take. They were all good men and truly as close a family tie as there can be. Lieutenant Skinner was one of the leaders of the whole Marine Recon Team program. A former enlisted man, he was a very successful officer and a true leader and friend.

This was a real downer. Lieutenant Skinner was a tough leader who was respected by all. He wouldn't order his men to do anything that he would not do. He was the rare superior in the military that you listened to and reacted when he spoke, but at the same time, you knew he was a true compatriot and friend.

"I can't believe it," I said. "Is his wife still in Tokyo?"

"Well, it's true," said Gunny to a shaken group. "His wife's back at home, and they had his funeral last week," said Sergeant Ryan. "All three of us attended, along with about twenty other marine and navy men he had served with. He was buried in his hometown in Iowa."

Sergeant Ryan suggested we all go to the hospital chapel as a group and pray for Lieutenant Skinner, Corporal Sawkowski, Private Harris, and their families. It was a somber time as we reflected on past times with our friends, and joined in prayer.

Back in the conference room, Captain Gordon filled us in on what we had accomplished on the last mission. We had rescued eleven American, five Australian, and two South Korean POWs and gotten them back to South Korea and freedom. Our people also determined there were more POWs in captivity elsewhere in North Korea through the interrogation of the hostile captives and discussions with the rescued men.

"You men also know that you have to go through a debriefing," said the captain, to our dismay, "so, consider yourself debriefed. I have the usual statements prepared for you to sign. All of you've been through this enough to know the rules." He plopped his briefcase onto the table and pulled out our "individual voluntary statements," which we all signed—in triplicate, of course.

The captain turned to me and said, "Doc, thank you for what you have done for our unit. We all had reservations when Lieutenant Skinner recruited you on your ship, knowing you had no training with our recon team. You had been through Field Medical Force training at Parris Island, and it's proved that you had some good experience at your other duty stations, so I guess Skinner knew what he was doing. He usually did. When you get back to your ship, you will be given some more information that we won't go into here. I understand you're being transferred to Oak Knoll Naval Hospital in Oakland for rehabilitation. Good luck and work hard. We'll be checking up on you."

"Thank you, sir. I figured you would, and that doesn't surprise me a bit. It was a great experience serving with you and your men, even Potter and Ryan sitting over there! Take care of yourselves and get you a good corpsman to keep you straight. By the way, when are you guys heading back to get those other men out of there? I sure would love to go, but I guess that's out of the question."

"You've served your time with the Marine Recon Team and you've done it well," said Captain Gordon. "As far as going back, we really don't know, but we're all itching to get them out. Maybe we can fill you in at a later time about a successful mission to free them. We can only hope. We'll see you later."

We said our good-byes, and the fearless threesome left. It was now chow time, so our group went to the mess hall for a good, hot dinner.

It was a quiet dinner until Reeves started laughing about all the crazy things that everyone had done on these unbelievable missions, and all of them seemed to revolve around Lieutenant Skinner. Surprise! Surprise!

For the next couple days, our little recon group ate together and shared our stories and gripes. Each of them was going back to the unit as soon as they were discharged for active duty. Then it was time for me to be transported back to Yokohama to catch the *Anderson* back to San Francisco.

The following morning, two soldiers and I were picked up in a Navy Suburban for the trip to Yokohama to board the *Anderson*. The soldiers had been hospitalized for illnesses, and they were being transferred back to the states for new duty stations.

During the ride, we stopped at a local restaurant for a breakfast stop for the driver. We tried their sweet rolls and some of the best coffee I had ever tasted. The rolls had a sweet-and-sour taste, but I didn't ask what was in them. I had learned to never ask what was in the food. That way, if it was good, I ate it. If it wasn't good, I didn't want to know what the ingredients were. It took us three hours to get to the ship, but we were in no particular hurry. The driver was able to drive us all the way to the gangplank. We thanked him for a fun ride and grabbed our bags. All I had was a small bag, because all my clothing was still onboard the ship, and I wasn't allowed to keep any of the marine gear.

I was greeted as I boarded the ship by several of my friends who were going ashore for a couple hours for a good meal and a couple drinks, I'm sure. I had to report in and get settled down to life aboard ship instead of sleeping in caves and under rock ledges in the rain and cold. The thought of a thin mattress, mattress cover, and a blanket sounded pretty good to me.

I went to the Master of Arms and handed him my papers. "Doc, it looks like you will travel in the sick bay as a patient this time instead of working for your bread and board. What happened to you anyway? You're walking and talking funny," asked the Boatswain's[2] Mate on duty.

"I ran into a doorknob while on vacation in Korea," I replied.

"Remind me not to go on liberty with you, Doc," he said. "You apparently don't know how to have fun. Go on up to sickbay. I'll bet

---

2   Pronounced BO-sun.

the chief will put you to work. He won't let you lie on your ass all the way across the Pacific."

The Boatswain was right. Chief Beagle put me back in the pharmacy, which was just open four hours a day. I could sit most of the time and fill the prescriptions and dispense the meds. That suited me just fine, because the pharmacy was my permanent duty station before I'd gone on TDY. No one had bothered to keep everything in order while I was gone, so I had plenty of work to do the rest of the day. The chief came back to the pharmacy and I asked, "Where is everyone? I haven't seen a corpsman except you since I came in this morning?"

"We knew you would be back today, so I let everyone go ashore. You've done nothing for the last six weeks, so it's time you earned your pay! Anyway, that's what Captain Gordon told me to tell you when he called our shoreline when we got in this morning."

"Do you know Captain Gordon?" I asked. "How did he know to call you?"

"Captain Gordon, Gunny Potter, and Sergeant Ryan stopped by the ship in San Francisco last month when they went to Lieutenant Skinner's funeral. They told me and Lieutenant Bowman [our ship's doctor] what had happened to you. No one else here knows where you were or what happened. As far as they know, you were trying to subdue a drunken sailor and were thrown back against a post, injuring your head."

"I didn't know you had met them; they didn't mention it to me, but I know why. They are a great bunch of guys. I learned a lot with them, and they really looked after us," I said. "They visited me and the other wounded in the hospital. The captain filled us in on everything that our unit did and the outcome of the mission."

"Here's something else they didn't tell you, and you will not repeat this to anyone: you were awarded two Purple Heart medals, the Korean Presidential Citation medal, a couple other medals that went with it, and above all, you were recommended for a Bronze Star medal. For the time being, you will not wear these medals, and they will not appear on your regular DD-214 until the missions you participated in are declassified and made public. As far as I know, you are the only person on this ship with a top-secret clearance. The only reason *I* was told is that Dr. Bowman and I are your senior chain of command, and Captain Gordon made us party to your official debriefing. You have signed your statement; so neither Dr. Bowman, you, nor I will discuss this matter again. Any questions?"

"I don't think so, Chief. I think you covered everything pretty well. All this is a surprise to me. I was told about the Purple Heart medal, and someone said it was awarded to me and pinned to my pillow in the Yokosuka Naval Hospital, but I don't remember seeing it. There's a lot I don't remember. Thanks for telling me all this," I said as we shook hands. That was the last time he mentioned my absence from the ship or the reason for it.

A few minutes later, Dr. Bowman came in and asked me how I was doing. He took me to a treatment room and examined my back, shoulders, and neck. "It all looks good. There are still several small pieces of shrapnel in your back, but I'd just leave them alone. They are doing no damage. You did a great job. Now we need to get you to Oak Knoll when we get back home and get you some speech and mobility therapy. Now, get back to work," he said with a laugh.

So that was the other information Captain Gordon had told me I would be given. *Enough of that!* I went back to the pharmacy and saw that I was out of boxed APCs, PBZs, and bottles of ETH[3] cough syrup—*looks like I will be working more than four hours today.* This busy work was appreciated for the trip back to San Francisco. I decided to go back to the Corpsman's Lounge to greet the other corpsmen as they came back aboard.

It was good seeing everyone, and I had to field a lot of questions about my injury. I stuck to the head-injury-by–a-drunken-sailor story. There were two new corpsmen who had been permanently transferred that I met last time on-ship. This told me that I would not be coming back here after I got out of the hospital.

The loudspeaker let us know that it was time to get ready to get underway. We all went to our assigned duty stations, but suddenly, I had a partner in the pharmacy, so I knew who my replacement was. Hospital Corpsman Second Class Joe Mission introduced himself and said he was assigned to work with me so he could learn the routine in the pharmacy. The first thing I showed him was how to secure all bottles, water jugs, and all other gear for sea. Within two hours, we were underway. I soon learned that I had to walk with a cane aboard ship.

Thirty minutes out, I started to get dizzy, but was not sick to my

---

3 Elixir of Turpin Hydrate.

stomach. I could hardly walk, and my eyesight was getting fuzzier by the minute. At first, I thought I might be getting seasick, but that was not the case. Joe took me back to our lounge and went after Dr. Bowman.

That's all I remember until I woke up two hours later in the sickbay with Dr. Bowman, two nurses, and three or four corpsmen. I looked around and said, "I know I'm not dead, because you don't look like angels to me."

"He's okay now," said Dr. Bowman. "He's at least seeing now. Your equilibrium is out of whack, and you are going to have to stay where you are a little longer until the IV is completed."

I didn't even know there was one running. After a couple hours, they got me up to go to dinner with them. I made it to the mess hall and got my tray to the table. I ate about half the meal, and the dizziness started all over again. Everyone moved out of the way and had me lie down on the bench and close my eyes, which helped. Then Joe got me back to the sickbay and put me to bed again. Dr. Bowman came in and told me to stay put until he could check me out and find out what was going on.

At 2200 hours, Dr. Bowman came back in and told me he had been in his stateroom reading my medical file. "Now I understand a little more about your dizzy spells. I knew you were having mobility issues, but that was a very traumatic hit you took. They probably should have held you in the hospital a couple more weeks, but they did not want you to fly back to the States, better to go back by ship. You are suffering from an equilibrium imbalance, and as soon as you get your sea legs back, you should be able to handle this. I'm still not going to call this seasickness," he said laughing. "Of course, all the other guys will, I'm sure! I want you to stay in the sickbay for a couple days and work in the pharmacy only if you feel like it. Just don't try to do too much at any one time."

This equilibrium thing kept bothering me occasionally, and I managed to sleep in the sickbay all the way back to San Francisco. The cane really helped getting around the ship. Headaches became frequent, but I was used to having those. They were coming more and more often, affecting my daily activities and keeping me awake some nights. I didn't say much about them because I had enough going on. I did work a bit, getting Joe acclimated to running the pharmacy and showing him all the elixirs that we mixed, all the compounds we prepared, and offering some shortcuts on filling gelatin capsules. Yes, we did all that by hand—it's not that many years ago, my children! I also showed him all the daily, weekly, and monthly reports we had to prepare on inventories, prescriptions filled, shortages, overages, orders submitted and received, etc., etc., and on and on.

When we crossed under the Golden Gate Bridge, I had mixed emotions about leaving my friends on the ship. This was my last trip on the *Anderson*. It was a good duty station, but all good things do come to an end. After we docked at Fort Mason, I had help packing my sea bag. My old shipmates Gene Barnes, Rick Lamp, and Bob Wilson helped get all my gear together, and I was ready to go. They carried my sea bag and satchel down the gangplank to the dock and helped me get loaded into the station wagon for my trip across the bay to Oak Knoll—Oakland Naval Hospital. I did not go by the sickbay to see everyone before I left. It was better that way.

Chapter 6

Rehabilitation

Oakland Naval Hospital is located in the hills above the Bay Area in Oakland, California, in the Oak Knoll area. The one-story wooden buildings are surrounded by trees and landscaped flower gardens, giving it a quiet, serene atmosphere. It's a good location for a hospital.

The sailor driving the gray, Navy station wagon drove me to the administration building for admission to the facility. He carried my bags in to Admissions and wished me a quick recovery as he walked out the door.

I was greeted by another voice from the past as I approached the desk. "Larry Gentry, what in the world are you doing here? I thought you were pounding the ground with the marines in Korea!"

"Well, that's the reason I'm here, Nolan," I said, shaking hands with Hospital Corpsman Third Class Louis Nolan, with whom I had been in hospital corps school at Great Lakes, and then he went to Camp LeJeune Naval Hospital when I did in 1955. "How in heaven's name did you know I was with the marines in Korea? Not many people are supposed to know about that."

"Easy enough. Lanny Young, that you got your med supplies from in Korea, has been in contact with a couple of us here. Lanny never misses out on anything; he always knows what's going on everywhere. You remember Scott Lewinsky, who was one of the instructors at Great Lakes—he's in charge of Medical Transportation here now. By the way, he just made Hospitalman Second Class last month. Anyway, Lanny told us about you and for us to expect you here for rehab."

So much for confidentiality! "I didn't even know he knew I was coming here, but I might have known that Lanny would be behind this. He was a lot of help in Korea when we went upcountry. He's still as crazy as ever, and the doctor there says he's still the lady's man."

Nolan laughed at that. "Lanny will always be a lady's man—in his own mind, anyway. Scott, Dr. Noblitz, and I are the only ones here that know your little secrets; so don't worry. I have to process your medical records, so I would have found out most of it anyway. Come on over here to this office and the clerk will get your paperwork completed. We have most of it done already."

"Miss Wilson, this is Corpsman Gentry I told you to expect. You already have his file." I entered the small room and sat down at the desk.

"Good morning, Miss Wilson," I said.

"Hello, Corpsman. This won't take long, and we will get you to your ward." After a few minutes, the paperwork was completed, and Miss Wilson took me to Louis's desk.

"I'll take you to your ward, which is just two buildings over. You'll like it here at Oak Knoll," he said as we strolled up the walkway lined with flowers between the buildings. "It is quiet and peaceful here. You will find a very relaxed atmosphere. They are not as strict militarily here as they were at LeJeune. Here you are! This is your new home."

We entered a long room full of windows, with about twenty beds on each side. It was bright and sunny, for sure. There were enough patients for about every bed, and I don't think I have heard so many radios and record players in one room in my life. Almost everyone had one playing, and they all seemed to be on different stations.

Louis took me to the desk and introduced me to Hospitalman Arby Harrington and the nurse, Ensign Teresa Deen. "Welcome to Oak Knoll," said Nurse Deen. "Harrington has your bed ready. Please, put your pajamas on, so we can get you settled in, and Dr. Youngson will examine you. Get your toiletries and other necessities from your bags, and we will then put the bags in storage. The doctor will decide when you can wear your uniform after all your tests are completed, but you are considered a ward patient until then."

I looked around, and all the patients nearby had smiles on their faces and seemed to be waiting for my reaction to the stern attitude of the nurse. "Thank you, Ensign," I said with a smile. "It's nice to meet you." I turned and followed Harrington to the other side of the ward to my bed. "Is she that matter of fact all the time, or does she just like to hear herself talk?" I asked him as we got to my bed.

"She just goes by the book and doesn't change from one day to the next. Just keep this to yourself, and don't try to talk back to her. She's really not bad to work with," he replied.

"I'll take your word for it. I just want to get well and get the heck out of here," I said.

I went into the head and changed into my PJs, robe, and slippers. It felt pretty good, but I would always rather be in uniform. I went back to my bed and put everything in the side table, which had a lock and key that really worked. I put the key on my dog tag chain. Now would be a good time to take a nap; a little afternoon sleep would be great. Just as I lay back on the bed, Harrington came over, "Doc, you need to come on with me. The doctors want to see you in Treatment Room 3 and get started on your work-up."

"A little sleep would have been good, but I'm here for a reason," I thought. As I started down the hallway, a doctor down the way said, "Corpsman Gentry, hold your arms straight out to the side and let me see you walk." I did as he asked, and I zigzagged down the hall.

"I can't walk straight toward one point. I seem to go from side to side," I said to the doctor.

"We're here to correct that and to do something about your speech patterns also," he replied.

As I reached Room 3, he said, "I am Dr. Youngson, and that is Dr. Noblitz." We shook hands around, and Dr. Noblitz said, "Did you have any mobility and/or speech deficiencies before your so-called accident?"

"No, sir, I didn't have any health problems, anything like this before."

Lieutenant Donald L. Youngson, MD, was assigned as the ward doctor and was available to us daily. Commander Kimball Noblitz, MD, was a neurologist and neurosurgeon who served several navy hospitals.

The examination, tests, and lab work took over two hours. I was then told that I would receive a battery of tests and examinations over the next week or so. "Yours is not an uncommon occurrence in cases of explosive force trauma such as you experienced. We know you cannot reveal many specific details, but explain in general the trauma as you remember it. Tell us whether you remember the explosion itself and what you remembered afterwards."

"I don't remember the explosive force that hit me, but there were four or five mortar shell explosions that occurred prior to my being hit. My first recollection afterwards was when I woke up in a hospital bed with two IVs going. I then noticed I was strapped to the bed. That may have been about a week after I was hit. I did not recall the combat scene until I discussed it with one of the marines in the hospital that was wounded when I was. It came back clearly after that."

"It's rare that anyone remembers anything after being hit in a similar manner. Your slurring speech and mobility problems are to be expected in cases such as this. Your speech will come back pretty much on it's own without anything more than some speech therapy. We'll have to determine whether surgery will be indicated in correcting your walk pattern, but don't dwell on that. We have a lot of testing to perform yet," Dr. Noblitz said. He had been counting the scars on my back and shoulders while we were talking, "You are one lucky, young man."

"Yes, I am. As I was told, there were several that were not as fortunate as I. We lost some, but we also gained several POWs and MIAs because of our activities back there. We were privileged to have been a part of that."

The tests went on for another three weeks. Dr. Noblitz immediately got me started on speech therapy, and I hated it. But, guess what? My speech started improving in a matter of days, except when I got a little nervous or excited. However, after I was there a month or so, I started losing my balance and falling to the floor, daily at first and then more often. Dr. Youngson restricted me to the ward and to a wheelchair when I had to leave the ward. He wanted me to take my meals in the ward, but I went to the dining room with the other guys for them.

Early one morning, Dr. Noblitz appeared at my bedside and awoke me before anyone had gotten up. "I want to observe you at different times today to see if there's any difference in your mobility when you're rested and after a day of activity as you begin to tire. Now, get up slowly and go about your usual activities."

I got out of bed and put on my robe and slippers and started to the head. After walking about ten feet, I staggered and fell backwards while trying to gain my balance.

"Get him in a wheelchair, let him take care of everything and get ready for breakfast. Corpsman Gentry, eat a good breakfast and we will run some tests that we haven't run yet. And stay in the wheelchair—please."

I laughed nervously and said, "Yes, sir. I guess it's not getting any better."

Dr. Noblitz transferred me to another ward, where he had his office, and restricted me to a wheelchair, ordering me to not walk without assistance.

Lieutenant Martha Donovan was the nurse on this ward. "Corpsman Gentry," she said as I was wheeled in, "welcome to our ward. You're assigned to this second bed here and can place your gear in the bedside table and lock up your valuables. You should keep your key in a safe place. Stay close by your bed. Dr. Noblitz wants to see you shortly. I'll let you know when he's ready, so relax and let me know if you need anything. We'll have you up and going in no time at all."

"That's what I wanted to hear," I replied.

The next two weeks were a whirlwind of testing of all kinds. It tired me out, but I was not sleeping very well. Then Dr. Noblitz told me that he knew what was causing my problem with walking, and he wanted to discuss surgery. "Surgery will take care of your mobility issue. It's a simple procedure to relieve pressure on nerves that will only take a matter of forty-five minutes or so and certainly not more than two hours at the very most. I've performed this surgery many times and am confident that you'll experience positive results. Do you have questions?"

"That sounds good to me. No, I don't have any questions at this time, except when do you expect to get this done?"

Dr. Noblitz smiled and said, "That's the question I wanted. I've already scheduled it for 0600 hours tomorrow—on the condition you were ready. I think you're ready! It is now time to get on with it, but I want you to know that this isn't a quick fix. You'll notice some improvement in a day or two, but I'll be honest, you're looking at three to five months of rehab, if not more. The positive results I referred to are based on how much hard work you're willing to put into this."

"I'll put it this way, Doctor: you do your part, and I'll do my part to show my appreciation. I'm tired of sounding and looking like a drunken sailor," I said, laughing all the while.

He laughed too and shook my hand, saying, "It sounds as if we have a partnership, one doc to another!"

On the way back to my bed, I was hoping I had made the right decision. Before long, the corpsman came in and shaved the back of my head and painted it red. "We'll bring you a light dinner this evening, and you can have nothing to eat or drink after 2200 hours tonight. You can only have water to drink, but you can have all you want before 2200. We'll start your meds with your evening meal. Get plenty of rest, because you'll not be allowed to sit up for twenty-four hours after surgery. Your equilibrium will be upset by the surgery, and you'll need all your energy. That's all I have for now. Do you have any questions for me?"

"No, it sounds like you covered everything. You said all I could drink was water, so there's no sense asking for a beer or two. By the way, you didn't paint a white bull's eye on the back of my head, did you?"

He laughed and said, "No to both, no beer and no bull's eye. Get some rest, because the team from the OR will come in around 0500 hours. The night corpsman will start your IV around 0430 hours. Get some rest; you've been through a lot the last couple weeks, but we're going to get this thing under control ASAP."

The operation came and went. I remember very little for about a two-week period. My equilibrium was in turmoil, for sure. Dr. Noblitz called me to his office two weeks after the surgery. "Corpsman Gentry, you've had a rough two weeks, but you're turning the corner now. The x-rays we took two days ago show that we accomplished what we were after. You will now be starting physical therapy. We will start off with something we haven't done much before by starting your PT in a swimming pool, walking in the water. The water will help you lift your legs and support you while wearing a life vest. There will be another corpsman in the water with you guiding your movements."

That all sounded good to me, but to tell you the truth, I didn't even remember anyone taking the x-rays. I also found out that they had moved my bed into a "quiet" room for nearly a week, because I was evidently having bad dreams or nightmares and keeping the other patients awake at night. Louis Nolan told me about that when he came by to check on me ever few days after the surgery. "They had you in a padded cell," as he liked to say. "Just wait until I tell Lanny and the others about that."

To that, I jokingly replied, "Just wait until I get my hands on my carbine and see who you tell." We had a lot of laughs, but none of this equilibrium thing was funny.

The PT in the swimming pool was fun, but it was harder work than the therapy in the gym and the workroom on the parallel walking bars. It was now October, 1957, and I was seeing progress every day. I had not been in the wheelchair in over a month and was walking everywhere I went. It was tiring to do the exercises every day, but I kept increasing them and then going on walks. Nurse Donovan walked every day anyway, so I started walking with her. By the first of November, we were walking three miles a day. The therapist had now started me lifting weights in the gym, and I was feeling much better.

Just before Thanksgiving, Dr. Noblitz told me during a routine checkup that I was way ahead of his schedule, and if I wasn't careful, he was going to send me back to full-time duty. He had me assigned to work with other patients in the gym to show them what progress I had made. That gave me something to do to pass the time when I wasn't working out and kept me busy. I was invited to have Thanksgiving Dinner with some of my friends from the *Anderson*, but the doctors were still reluctant for me to leave the hospital just yet.

The next morning, I was called to Dr. Noblitz's office. He said that Dr. Bowman, the doctor from the *Anderson*, was on the telephone. He had told Dr. Noblitz that he and a couple others would pick me up on Thanksgiving and return me to Oak Knoll after dinner. Dr. Noblitz was agreeable to that, so I was going to get off the hospital campus for one day after all!

I was now walking three miles everyday with Nurse Donovan along with six or eight more corpsmen and nurses that had joined us. Donovan wanted to increase the mileage by December first, so I was going to have to dig down and see if I could keep up with them.

Thanksgiving Day came, and Dr. Bowman and his wife picked me up. We went to a restaurant in San Francisco, and there were about fifteen corpsmen, nurses, and doctors from the *Anderson*. It was good to see them all. Most of us had worked together nearly two years aboard the ship. There were questions about my injury, but I put them off with the same old story of getting knocked against a steel post and cracking my skull. My speech was so much better, with very little slurring or hesitation. I was walking straight for the most part, and my stamina was unbelievable, thanks to the daily walks with Nurse Donovan for the past two or three months. What did not show were the headaches that were nearly unbearable at times, but I didn't mention them.

"I think I'll have a steak instead of turkey for this Thanksgiving meal," I said. "I haven't had a real beef steak in about a year, just water buffalo." That brought a round of laughter.

"I remember you putting away several of those buffalo steaks at the Zebra Club," said Rick.

Then Bob spoke up, "Yeah, and you put away several bourbon-and-water drinks with those steaks too."

"This is the last time I'm hanging around this group; your memories are too good for me. Besides, if most of you can't remember anything, you'll just make up a story. And some of you can make up some good stories." It went on like that for three hours or more until I had to call it a day.

I stood up at the head of the table and raised my glass of water, "I want to thank all of you for a most memorable Thanksgiving. It's always good to spend holidays with your family, even if it's your extended family. You have all been … well, let's just leave it at that. Here's to you, and we'll always be family, and I thank you for a great day. I have to get back to Oak Knoll and get some rest. Let's make every effort to get together again as soon as we can. Aloha!" We shook hands and hugged and made the promises of many more reunions.

Lieutenant and Mrs. Bowman escorted me down the street to their car in the restaurant parking lot. "You got awfully tired in there, didn't you, Larry?" said Mrs. Bowman. "You lasted longer than I thought you were going to there for a while."

Dr. Bowman looked back at me, "You're having one of your headaches, aren't you?"

I grinned and replied, "Well, truth be told, I had a bad headache when I got up this morning, but I wasn't going to miss this day. Thank you both for giving me a ride and for a nice day all the way around."

It was a quiet ride back across the bridge to Oakland. It turned out that the Bowmans lived less than a mile from the hospital and did not have to go out of the way to pick me up. Dr. Bowman walked me back to my ward when we arrived and made sure I made it okay. He also told Nurse Deen about my headache before he left. So, I was back in the ward again, but that was one of the most enjoyable days I'd had for a long time. I slept the night through after I took my medications.

My recovery and rehabilitation moved faster with each passing day for the next several weeks. I spent the Christmas and New Year's holidays with occasional outings with different friends, but spent the nights in my bed at Oak Knoll. Then the first week in January, Dr. Noblitz moved me to one of the enlisted barracks and put me on light duty in his wards. "We need to get you back into your routine slowly. We'll start you slowly by giving out meds and keeping check on the patients, but no lifting or excessive bending over, for now. I think the headaches may lessen after you get back to work and take on more responsibility." In other words, he wanted to put me to work and keep my mind off my problems. Pretty smart. The ward duty continued for five weeks, four hours a day, and it did help me improve my communication with everyone.

My mobility was getting better each day as well. Lieutenant Donovan was still inviting me to walk with her daily, and that was probably helping me more than anything else. She set a schedule of walking three miles on Mondays and Tuesdays, four miles on Wednesdays, three miles on Thursdays, and five miles on Fridays. We did have a half-mile track for walking and running. Neither of us did very much walking on weekends. The doctors didn't allow me to jog or run during treatment, only the scheduled walks. I would get headaches when I tried to jog, so I didn't do that anymore. Almost every day, there were around twenty patients and staff walking with us. The doctors were now recommending patients for Lieutenant Donovan to add to the walkers.

The second week of February, Dr. Noblitz had me stop by his office after one of my shifts. "We're going to find a way to stop your headaches. I can tell they are coming more often. You'll not be working on the ward for a while. I want you to discontinue your walking regimen until further notice. There's a new test, more of an observation really, that will begin today. I don't know if you are familiar with our 'sleep lab,' but you'll be sleeping in a darkened room while being monitored. We've been told by your ward nurses and corpsmen that you're restless in your sleep. They also tell me you're apparently having nightmares. We need to find out what's going on in your head."

"Good luck with that," I laughed with him. "I know I'm having bad dreams and wake up several times each night reliving my experiences in Korea. The so-called sleeping pills I've been getting just make things worse. When I don't take the pills, I still don't sleep much, but I don't have those disturbing dreams as bad either."

And so it was: two weeks of sleeping in a darkened room with a window on one side and the faint glow of red lights. They had microphones hanging over my bed. They tried wiring sensors to my head, but I kept getting tangled up in the wires, so that just lasted two or three nights. When I would wake up in the middle of the night and couldn't get back to sleep, I would talk and tell jokes to whoever was listening to me, but they never talked back. I don't know if they laughed at the jokes or not. Dr. Noblitz did tell me later that I had an interesting since of humor, so he must have enjoyed the recordings.

After the two weeks of monitored sleep tests with my usual medication, the doctor changed to new sleeping pills every four nights. Dr. Noblitz tried four new medications under the controlled sleeping conditions. Then he moved me to the ward and had me try the sleeping pills while sleeping there. This went on through the month of March, and by the second week of April, Dr. Noblitz had decided on the pill that worked best for me. I agreed with him, and he had also reduced my meds for the headaches. I was sleeping better and feeling better, with milder headaches.

"I think you're on the right track now. As a matter of fact, I've cleared you for active duty effective May 1. Tomorrow, you will appear before a board of five doctors that will examine you and ask you a battery of questions. This will be the final authority to clear you to go back to duty. This is customary in cases such as yours, and they can make three recommendations: One. They can clear you for active duty. Two, They can recommend you for further treatment. Or three. They can recommend you for a medical discharge. My best feeling is that you'll be recommended for active duty."

The session with the doctors lasted for two hours and was not unpleasant. When they started asking questions, it seemed I was being questioned by five lawyers asking the same thing five different ways. On toward the end of the session, on one question, I said, "I think I can remember how I answered that the last two times." The doctor looked at me sternly before he started laughing and said, "I think we've asked you enough questions today. After two hours, you're able to stay ahead of us. You're dismissed." They said they would give their report to Dr. Noblitz the next day.

"Thank you, sirs," I replied.

The following day, Dr. Noblitz told me the doctors had cleared me for active duty and wished me luck. "Evidently you made a good impression on them. The sessions usually last for three to five hours," he said.

"Three to five hours sounds like torture to me," I said, "but I thank them for releasing me. I don't mean to sound ungrateful, but I am ready to move on to another duty station. Thank you for all you have done, Dr. Noblitz."

"You're welcome, Corpsman. Good luck, and we appreciate your help while you were here. I'll forward a letter to the doctor at your new duty station. Continue your present regimen and consult with your doctor if any changes occur. You will be fine, Doc."

My orders came in the following Tuesday. I was to report to the USS *General D. I. Sultan*, TAP 120, which would be docked at Fort Mason in San Francisco on May 1, 1958. The *Sultan* was an Army Transport Ship assigned to the Military Sea Transport Service (MSTS). MSTS is responsible for transporting troops and dependents to duty stations and back to homeports throughout the world. The *Sultan*, just like the *Anderson*, was assigned to the Pacific Ocean out of Fort Mason.

Two days before I left Oak Knoll, I went by to see Lieutenant Donovan and thank her for all her help. "I enjoyed all our walking sessions. You had trouble keeping me headed in the right direction at first, but you succeeded in straightening me out. I will be going back aboard an MSTS ship on May 1. I will be on the *Sultan* this time."

She gave me a hug and said, "I wish you the best of luck. You'll enjoy your new assignment. I served on the *Sultan* for two years. I think Lieutenant Secunda is still their medical doctor. The *Sultan* is the most unusual situation I've ever been in. It's an army ship with wooden decks; it has a merchant marine crew, and there are twenty-six navy personnel on board. Two are the ship's captain and executive officer, twelve are doctors and nurses, and the remaining twelve are hospital corpsmen."

"Thanks again, Lieutenant; you played a great part in my rehabilitation," I told her as I left. "It was my pleasure, Larry," she said.

When I went to Louis Nolan's office, he had his feet on the desk reading reports on a clipboard. "Off and on there, Corpsman," I said out loud.

He jumped up saying, "Don't come in here like that. I nearly jumped out of my skin," he laughed. "I hear you're going back to sea. Can't you land a job on land?"

"It seems I'm just destined to be a real sailor. The last time I was at sea, I ended up as a ground-pounder, but I have my doubts that will happen again."

When I left Nolan's office, I then went by to see Scott Lewinsky. He had also served on the *Sultan* and said I would enjoy it. "Your sleeping quarters are four-bed staterooms with your own head. There's a porthole in each stateroom, so you can tell when it's night or day. Best of all, there's a small dining room for the corpsmen, with real tablecloths and real china. A waiter will take your menu order for each meal. I think you'll enjoy your time aboard the *Sultan*." I thought he was kidding and having fun with me, but it turned out that he was telling the truth.

On May 1, I left Oak Knoll for my new duty assignment. Lewinsky, being in charge of medical transportation there, arranged for me to ride in a new Buick four-door sedan to Fort Mason. It was the CO's car, but he was out of town, and no one would know the difference. No one but me, that is. Thanks, Scott!

CHAPTER 7

BACK TO SEA

The USS *General Daniel I. Sultan*, TAP 120 was docked at the same pier at Fort Mason where I last saw the USS *General A. E. Anderson*, TAP 111. The *Sultan* and the *Anderson* were troop ships with the designation AP from Auxiliary "All Purpose" cargo ships, I've been told. The T designation was added when they were assigned to the Military Sea Transport Service (MSTS). There were several hundred of these ships and each had a different number assigned. When we pulled up to the dock in the Buick, two seamen came over to get my bags. They were surprised when an enlisted man got out of the car. One of them looked in the car to see if there was anyone else. "No, I'm the only passenger. It's my father's car," I said without a smile, "but I do need help with my bags, if you will." They did carry my sea bag and duffle bag up the gangplank, but they left them for me on the quarterdeck.

I reported in to the officer of the day, "Request permission to come on board, sir," I said with a salute. The ensign returned my salute, "Permission granted." I turned to the yeoman and waited while I was checked in. The yeoman told me, "Everything is in order, Doc. You can leave your sea bag behind the counter for now. It is two decks up to the sickbay."

I carried my small bag up the ladders to the sickbay, where I met Hospital Corpsman Second Class John Williams. "Welcome aboard, Gentry," he said when I handed him my orders. "Have you been aboard ship before?"

"Yes, I was on the *Anderson* until last summer. I was TDY to a marine recon unit a couple times from the *Anderson*. Then I was in the hospital at Oak Knoll since July or August. Before the *Anderson*, I was at Parris Island Marine Depot and then Camp LeJeune Naval Hospital after leaving corps school at Great Lakes. It's good to be back on duty."

"Sounds like you have had some good experiences during your first three and a half years. It looks like you and I have something in common, but we'll discuss it later. What were your assignments on the *Andy*?" That sounded strange, but he said we would discuss later what we had in common.

I replied, "I started on the ward and the sick-call treatment room, but for the last six months, I was in charge of the pharmacy and had a staff of just one—me."

"Let's go get your bags and see if we can find you a place to bunk. Everyone else is ashore right now. I'm the only one on duty, but I've been home on leave for thirty days, so I let the others have the day to relax. We sail tomorrow at 1000 hours, so I guess they need one last beer before we head to Japan. By the way, we go to Japan by way of Honolulu. Can you handle that?"

That did sound good. "Yeah, I haven't been there in over a year. I could use some of the South Pacific sunshine. It sounds great."

We went by the quarterdeck and picked up my sea bag. "Your room is just on the other side of the ship from here," Williams said. "You will be rooming with Dental Technician Third Class Larson and Hospital Corpsman Third Class Allison. There are four beds in each room, but there are only three of you in there right now. Here it is." He opened the door, and I could not believe the four-bed stateroom with our own bathroom and shower! We had lockers where we could actually hang our uniforms and clothing. There was shelving and a keyed door for securing our valuables. The mattresses looked to be eight inches thick.

"Just across the passageway amidships is the enlisted dining room. We have good food with waiters to serve us on white tablecloths and china just like the officers. At 2100 hours, they set up a buffet in our lounge with meats, cheeses, and snack foods. By the way, they bake all their own bread. Everything is different on this ship because we have a merchant marine crew, including the cooks. Best duty I've had. After you get unpacked and stow your gear, come on up to the sickbay and we'll have time to fill you in on everything."

I took an hour or so to get everything the way I wanted and looked around to see what all I could find. It was an old ship, dating way back before World War II, but it was totally in shipshape. All the outside decks were weathered and well-worn wooden decks, but looked great. After finding my way up to the sickbay, I found Williams in our little lounge. He was sacked out on one of five leather sofas and appeared sound asleep.

"Come on in and have a seat, Gentry. I figured that was you walking around from door to door trying to find me. Tell me, were you recruited by Lieutenant Skinner a year or so ago to serve with the recon team?" Appearances can be deceiving.

"How did you know? I didn't think anyone here would know about that," I said with amazement.

"No one else here knows about it but me. I'm the corpsman you replaced. The day we were leaving San Francisco, I was backed over by a taxi on the docks and broke my leg. I was leaving Oak Knoll late last summer when they brought in the corpsman who was wounded in Korea serving with Skinner's team." That would be me. "Have you heard from Skinner, Potter, Ryan, or any of them?"

"Oh, my God. You don't know about Skinner," I said before I thought how I was about to break the news to him."

"What do you mean I don't know about Skinner?" he said, jumping up.

I said, "Sit down, Williams. After our last mission, Skinner was riding in a taxi in Tokyo on the way to meet with his wife and was hit by a truck, killing the lieutenant and the taxi driver. He didn't know what hit him!" We just sat there for a moment looking at each other with tears in our eyes, then he slammed his hands down to the couch and jumped up.

"I can't believe it. After all we went through in Korea, and he gets it in a damned taxi. Was there anyone else lost while you were with them?" he asked.

"Well ... on the first trip, Private Dawson was killed near Pyonggang Airfield. On the next trip, Corporal Mattingly and Private McMartin got it outside Kaesong. Then Corporal Park, the South Korean soldier, died near Sariwon. Next were Corporal Sawkowski and Private Harris, who were killed just south of Pyongyang when we rescued the POWs. That's when I was wounded; I don't know too much about what went on there."

"Oh man, that's unbelievable. I knew Mattingly, Park, Ski, *and* Harris. I just can't believe it. But we lost five on one mission and didn't get to bring any of them back, but we know where they are. This is too much to take in at one time. Just don't say anything about any of this to the others up here. Dr. Secunda is the only one up here that knows about my duty with the recon team, so let's keep it among us. We'll have to look up Potter and Ryan when we get back to Japan." We agreed to give that a try when we got to Yokosuka.

We went to my first meal on the *Sultan*. Since we were in port, we ate in the crew's galley, and if this was any example of the food we would have, I was looking forward to our next meals. That was the best beef pot roast with vegetables I'd eaten since I left home, and the huge biscuits were just like homemade … well, almost.

Late that afternoon, the crew started coming back onboard from liberty in San Francisco and the Bay Area. I met the other corpsmen, the doctors, and the nurses. Lieutenant Commander Secunda came in, and I said, "Dr. Secunda, Lieutenant Martha Donovan from Oak Knoll sends her regards. She said she'd served with you, and told me what a great person you were."

He laughed as he replied, "Gentry, I can see already that you're either a diplomat or a con artist—come to think of it, there's not much difference between the two. How is Martha these days?"

"She's doing really well. She's still walking miles and miles each day. As a matter of fact, her walking regimen contributed greatly to my mobility recovery. I probably wouldn't be back on duty without her help. By the way, Dr. Noblitz, the neurologist that treated me, said he would send you a letter about my treatment."

"Dr. Noblitz called me a couple days ago and filled me in. Looks like you're doing okay, considering what you went through."

"Yes, sir," I replied, "I've been very fortunate with the initial treatment I received in Japan, and then what Dr. Youngson and Dr. Noblitz did for me at Oak Knoll. It's great to be here." I then met my roommates, Dental Technician Third Class Tommy Larson and HM3 Howard Allison, who had just gotten back from Fisherman's Wharf in San Francisco. They had eaten at Trader Vic's, one of my most favorite restaurants anywhere. They told me they ate enough for all of us. I guess that would do for now. Chief Hanes called us all together and asked us to meet in the hospital office at 1930 hours, after we had eaten and everyone had settled down.

Chief Hospital Corpsman Bart Hanes had been in the navy for thirty years, and this was his last cruise before retirement. He had joined the navy the day he turned eighteen and was sworn in one week later. He said he started out as a deck hand for about a year and that it didn't take him long to start looking for a better way to make a living on a ship than chipping paint or working in a steamy, oily engine room. He applied for a transfer to train to be a Pharmacist Mate three times before it was approved. After working as an apprenticeship, he went to a four-week school, and it was all history from there. He made Chief Hospital Corpsman (HMC) in sixteen years and enjoyed a good career. He was married and had four children back home in Oakland.

After another good meal, we all gathered in the hospital office. There were five corpsmen including the chief, and three nurses came in also. "Well, this is the medical team for this trip. I asked the nurses to come in on this meeting because there are going to be over a hundred military dependents—wives and children—not to mention over four thousand marines going to Japan," said Chief Hanes, adding, "We will pick up about one-fourth of them in Honolulu on the way outbound. You have all met Corpsman Gentry who is assigned to treatment-room and pharmacy duties. He will also be assisting in the emergency room when needed there. I have posted schedules on the bulletin board, but there will be no night assignments until patients are admitted to the sickbay overnight. Okay, that's it until 0700 hours tomorrow. Rest up and be ready for the rush."

There was a lot of activity on the dock that night with the supplies being loaded almost till morning. At least our room was on the portside of the ship, opposite the docks, so the lights and noise didn't bother our night's sleep that much.

I was sleeping so well when reveille sounded at 0530 that I sat up and could barely remember where I was for a couple moments. Howard and Tommy were already up and dressed. Tommy had been called out for a dental emergency at 0400, and Howard had gone with him to assist. A deck hand had been smashed in the mouth by a swinging boom and broken a couple teeth. "You slept through this one, Larry, but you get the next one," said Howard. "I guess you remember how it is when men and machinery are working together."

I looked up at them and replied, "I surely do. And it won't get any better when all those Gyrenes start hitting their heads and shins on the steel hatches."

They both laughed saying, "We can tell you definitely have been on a troop ship before."

After a good breakfast, we went up to the hospital and started getting everything ready for sick call when everyone was onboard and we had gotten underway. We did our preliminary inventory of supplies, meds, and instruments. Hospital Corpsman Second Class Williams came in and made sure we had it all stowed for sailing. You've never seen so much checking and double-checking, but that's what it takes to provide medical care for over 4300 troops, dependents, and ship's crew. I was surprised at the modern facilities on such an old ship, but we were well equipped.

By 0600, the troops were arriving on the docks and embarking by the rear gangplank. All the troop quarters were below decks, and some of them below the waterline. The bunks were steel pipe frames with canvas laced in and were hung twenty or so inches apart and about six bunks high. There's barely room to turn over. I wondered how many would be at first sick call trying to get admitted to the hospital so they didn't have to sleep below decks.

By 1010, everyone was aboard, all lines had been cast off, and we were backing out into the bay and ready to get underway. The tugs backed off and the ship shuddered as the huge propellers started turning, pushing us toward the Golden Gate Bridge and out to sea. As the ship glided under the Golden Gate, from our vantage point on the deck, it looked as if the masts and antenna were going to hit the bridge, but it really didn't even come close. After a half hour or so, the ship started the slow roll back and forth that really gets to some people, especially the troops below decks. That is not a pleasant place to be, until after the troops get their sea legs and their stomachs settle down. I've often wondered if it's not cruel and inhuman punishment that the first evening meal out of port is *always* greasy pork ribs. That was the sad truth. It seemed to be a waste of good food on the uninitiated landlubbers.

A couple of days later we are in Hawaii. We pulled into Pearl Harbor right by the Battleship USS *Arizona* that still sat under the water where it sank on December 7, 1941. You could see the smokestacks just below the surface and there were oil slicks on the water from the oil seeping from the ship's huge fuel tanks. That was a very sobering sight. "It has only been seventeen years since the merciless Japanese attack, but it seems like so much longer," I said to Tommy, Howard, and Hospital Corpsman Third Class Arlene Smythe, the only female corpsman onboard, as we slowly passed by the resting place for hundreds of sailors and marines.

It is noted that the oil slicks still appear on the water above the Arizona in Pearl Harbor in 2011, seventy years after the attack and the beginning of the United States' involvement in World War II.

Arlene said, "That was awful. I have heard that they are going to build a memorial over the *Arizona* as soon as they can raise enough money. They need to do something so no one will ever forget what happened here." We all agreed with her on that.

"We're only going to be in port for eight hours before we get underway again," said Chief Hanes, "so who's going ashore and who's got duty today?"

Chief Hanes and Williams told us they would take it today, since there were no patients in the hospital. The rest of us put on our dress whites and waited for the gangplank to be put in place, and we headed into Honolulu. We found a little restaurant in the suburbs that I had been to before. They had good food, cold beer, and a little band playing music. There was a native singer performing that some of us had heard before; he was an Air Force pilot home on leave who would one day become a household name: Don Ho. He was really good. We had a great meal, listened to the Hawaiian music, and gave the *flyboy* singer a hard time, but he kidded us *swab-jockeys* right back. We then went for a walk on the beach and, afterwards, reluctantly headed back to the *Sultan* before the gangplank would be pulled up. What an enjoyable day.

By nightfall, the sea was beginning to get a little choppy, and the clouds were rolling in rapidly. I was awakened after midnight by the ship rolling back and forth at a pretty good rate. Our beds were positioned cross ways, and it felt like I was standing on my feet one minute and on my head the next. "Hey, guys," I said, "what'd you people do to make the sea gods angry? I'll bet the troops are having a good time hanging onto those bunks below decks."

Howard laughed, "Yeah, and I'll bet they're having a hard time holding on to their dinners too!"

Tommy said, "That might not be too funny if you're on the bottom two bunks either." Neither of us laughed at that one.

"I don't know about you fellows," I said, "but I can see right now we won't get much sleep tonight. I've been through these storms too many times before. I'm going on up to the hospital before they have to send someone after us." Howard and Tommy agreed, so we put on our jeans and T-shirts and went on up.

"Glad to see you guys," said the chief. "Gentry, you and Allison go into the ER. There are four or five in there already that need sutures. Larson, go see if Dr. Dole is up yet; you have one in room 2 that Williams is working with who needs to get into your dental chair. It's going to be a busy night."

The nurses and Arlene came in, and we all got busy. We had four treatment rooms just off the ER, and they all had patients waiting for us. John and the chief had been going back and forth with each one controlling the bleeding. We started treating the patients, and most of them were marines who were not used to the small openings of the steel hatches. One of them had mashed fingers from one of the swinging steel doors closing on his hand. We had several troops and a few dependents come in needing something for seasickness, but we always had a few of them.

The storm lasted until after 1200 hours the next day, and the injured kept us busy almost constantly. We had a couple more storms on this trip, but we did not have but a couple injuries on each of them. Evidently, they learned how to cope with life at sea.

On the fourth day out of Honolulu, a message came from the bridge that we had received an SOS from a Greek freighter about fifty miles away, and their captain appeared to be having an appendicitis attack. They did not have a doctor onboard. Dr. Secunda went up to the bridge and, upon communicating with the Greek first mate, determined the symptoms did indicate the diagnosis could be correct. Our captain started making arrangements to meet the ship and transfer their captain over to our ship. *That* was interesting.

Later that afternoon, we rendezvoused with the Greek ship and pulled alongside, steaming in the same direction at a slow rate of speed. The boatswain's mate fired a line from our deck to the deck of their ship. Then the Greeks pulled a large line across to support a *bosun's chair*—a device used to suspend a person from a rope to perform work on a mast usually—and transport the ailing Greek captain from their ship to the *Sultan*. This was a two-hour operation and was exciting to watch. The captain was dunked in the water two times, but at least the water was not very cold. When we finally got him onboard, we carried him to the hospital. He was evidently in a lot of pain.

Dr. Secunda had the operating room ready, and he told the OR nurses and corpsmen to start scrubbing, while we were prepping the captain for surgery. Williams drew some blood for the lab work-up, while Howard and I shaved and "painted" the affected area with a red disinfectant. The captain was already in his pajamas, but we had to get dry PJs for him after his dunking during the transfer. The surgery was a success, and Dr. Secunda said the appendix was really hot and could have ruptured at any time.

After we got the captain awake and stabilized, we wheeled him to his room. It was evident while we were trying to get him into bed that he did not speak English, and of course, none of us could speak Greek. Everyone was laughing, especially the captain, by the time we got him settled in. He was holding his stomach with both hands and still laughing. "Okay, everyone take it easy. We don't want him to bust a stitch laughing at us clowns," I said. "I'll take the first watch with him. He needs to get some rest." I turned to the captain and made a motion to him to go to sleep, but he said "No, no," and made the motion of drinking water.

I gave him some crushed ice to munch on, and it seemed to satisfy him—for the time being anyway. Dr. Secunda came in with one of the merchant marine crewmen who spoke Greek. That made everything much better, especially for the doctor.

The captain was up and walking the next morning when I got back to the hospital. He smiled and nodded "good morning" to us with a big smile. He appeared to be feeling pretty good on the morning following surgery. Dr. Secunda ordered breakfast for the captain, and he was ready to eat. His recovery was rapid, and our ship's captain provided quarters in the officer's country, the private area reserved for officers, for the Greek captain for the remainder of the trip. Two or three times, the Greek captain ate with us in our dining room. He was learning a few English words—or as he put it, "I say American words." He was a lot of fun, but I would like to know what he said to us most of the time!

The rest of the trip to Japan was relatively uneventful. The sick call lasted two or three hours each day, but that was not an unusual thing. That was the highlight of the day for the troops below decks. Those with a cough were sure to come to sick call. Most of them would ask for a small bottle of cough syrup, which was elixir of terpin hydrate (ETH)—or more commonly known as *GI Gin*. We were careful about prescribing the ETH for coughs, because some of them wanted a bottle each day. Elixirs contain just too much alcohol.

The day we pulled into Japan, our Greek friend came by to tell all of us "Goom-by" and shook hands with each one of us. The translator from the crew said he wanted all of us to come ashore with him so he could have a drink with us. Dr. Secunda said we could not all go ashore with him, but then he placed a fifth of Scotch whiskey on the table. "Why don't we all just have a drink right here?"

The captain laughed and said, "Good deal, Okay?"

"Okay!" everyone said, and Williams came out with some two-ounce medicine glasses, and we all toasted the captain and he toasted us. He thanked us for his good treatment and wished us well.

We entered Tokyo Bay and docked at Yokohoma. There was a huge crowd awaiting our arrival, mostly husbands and fathers of the dependents who were now starting to disembark. The troops were disembarking from the aft gangplank. We were busy cleaning up the hospital and stowing everything in its place. When everything was shipshape, the doctor cleared us for a two-day liberty ashore. There were medical facilities available for the crew on the docks, so we shut down the hospital for forty-eight hours.

Williams had made a couple ship-to-shore calls to Gunnery Sergeant Potter and arranged a meeting with him, Ryan, and Reeves. He did not tell them that I was with him. We finally left the ship and got a ride over to Potter's office. We walked into the lobby and went on past the private in the outer office, motioning for him to not say anything. I pushed Potter's door open and shouted "Attention on deck!" Potter looked up and Ryan and Reeves were also getting to their feet.

"I'm not believing this! Doc, where in the world did you drop in from?" asked Gunny. All three came over and shook hands and hugged both of us.

"What did we do to deserve both of you at one time?" asked Reeves, "We thought both of you were out of commission."

Ryan turned me around and looked at the back of my head saying, "It's a damned good thing they hit you in the head or you would have been dead by now."

"Thanks a lot, you guys," I said. "It's evident you don't have anything to do. It's not surprising to find you sitting around wasting taxpayers' money."

Williams chimed in, "Isn't that the truth. I thought Captain Gordon would have you doing something worthwhile by now."

After we kidded each other for about twenty minutes, Potter said, "The truth of the matter is, Captain Gordon is now *Major* Gordon, and he has given us a job to do. It's a shame you two can't stick around for a month or so. The major has information that some more POWs have been seen near Sariwon. We will have a team ready to go in about ten days to two weeks—as soon as this is confirmed and we can get more details."

The door opened and in walked the new major. "Well, I'll be damned. Two of the worst corpsmen I've ever seen have come back from the dead. How are you two doing?"

We shook hands with Major Gordon, and I said, "That makes two references to the dead since we've been here. I don't know if I want to have anything to do with this crowd or not."

Williams said, "Gentry and I are both on the same ship now. I got out of the hospital last summer, and he just got out a couple weeks ago."

We had a good reunion and it was evident they had a lot to discuss. The major said, "I'll tell you what, men. Give us a half hour here, and we'll all go get a meal—and I'm buying with the big raise I got with my promotion."

We accepted, "Thanks, Major, we'll wait for you in the outer office."

We took a seat in the lobby and talked about how we would like to go with them to search for the POWs. "I guess we had better be careful what we ask for," I said. "Come to think of it, I've been on four missions, and I didn't volunteer for any of them."

Williams replied, "Come to think of it, I've been on five missions, and I didn't ask to go on any of them either. That's the *new, volunteer Navy/marine Corps* for you. It may not be a good idea for us to go on this dinner with them, but we have two days and I'm hungry."

I looked at my watch, "I guess we had better stick around and go with them. It's already been forty minutes since we came out here. There's no telling what they've run into, but I think we'll wait and get that free meal from Gordon."

After an hour and twenty minutes, they came out and the major said, "We left it up to Potter to tell us when our half hour was up, so here we are; let's go find a good steak."

John looked at them and said, "We didn't really expect you to get out here that soon. But I'm ready to eat." We all went out front and the major had an unmarked Suburban that we loaded into, and he took us out to a very nice restaurant. It was a thirty-minute drive to the restaurant, and we were the only military there except for two navy officers at the bar.

We all had steaks, baked potatoes, a salad, and a couple or four drinks. It was a Japanese restaurant, but the American influence showed in the menu. I held up a drink and said, "Congratulations, Major. Thank you for our meal, and we look forward to attending the banquet when you make general."

He held up his glass, "I'll drink to that, and you can rest assured, if I ever make general, you and your cohorts here are certainly invited."

It was a good reunion, and we had a toast and round of memories for the men we had lost from our teams. They had been on two missions in the past several months just for reconnaissance and did not have any casualties, but did come back with some good information, whatever it was. They had a veteran corpsman who had accompanied them several times before with them on these two trips. He was no longer active with the team and had transferred to Parris Island as a field medical force instructor.

We left the restaurant, and Major Gordon took us back to the base. "You two can stay in the enlisted quarters. The gunny will make the arrangements for you for tonight. Then you are on your own tomorrow. Thanks for everything, and I enjoyed the dinner that I paid for."

We laughed at him, and I said, "You're not going to let us forget you paid for that dinner, are you?"

"Nope!" he said with a big laugh.

Gunny, Ryan, and Reeves took us into the enlisted quarters and got us each a room in the Staff NCO quarters. "You guys have a good evening, and we'll see you for chow in the morning, if you get up in time," Ryan said.

We shook hands around and went to our respective rooms. I washed my face and got ready for bed. I turned on the radio and found some relaxing music. About the time I got into bed, there was a knock at the door. I got up, put on my pants, and opened the door. There stood Ryan and Reeves, who came right on into my room. "Hi Doc," said Ryan. "There's something we need to discuss. The reason we kept you waiting over an hour before dinner is that Major Gordon was on the phone with your ship's doctor about one or both of you joining back with our team for the next two months."

I looked at each of them and said, "I knew you gyrenes were up to no good. I just knew this was going to happen. But what did the doctor say? That's what I want to know."

"The doctor told the major that you both could be cleared for one of the missions, but that Williams could not be spared from the ship because of his role in the operating room, I believe it was."

I replied, "John is our only OR Tech and is really needed on the ship. I am one of three ward corpsmen and could be easily replaced. I just don't know if I am physically ready yet. I am feeling great, and the headaches have really subsided. I'm just surprised that I am being considered."

Reeves put his hand on my arm and said, "You have already been cleared by your doctor. Major Gordon and the gunny are going to tell you about this at breakfast tomorrow. They have already got it settled to their satisfaction. It looks like you have volunteered again, if you will accept it."

"The first thing that comes to my mind is to turn this down, if I can, but why would I? This is what I have been trained to do, and it seems they are confident in my abilities, no matter what I think. I just don't know."

Sergeant Ryan said, "That is exactly why Corporal Reeves and I came by here tonight, so you could have time to think about it before the major dropped it in your lap. You have always been straight with us, but don't say anything to John because he doesn't know about it yet. Just think about it, and we will see you at 0700 hours. I hope you can get some sleep."

It was a very long night. I tried to sleep, but it was hopeless. I finally got up and paced around the room. I was not upset or worried about the prospect of going on another mission—my biggest concern was whether I would be physically able to do the job. Who am I trying to kid?" I said, out loud to myself, "This is crazy. They will not want me to go on another mission after several months in the hospital. Ryan did say there was not another corpsman in the area with the training to join the team. Well, I did not have much training when I went on my first mission. But if the powers that be *are* confident I can perform the required duties, why not go along with them?"

I talked and talked to myself and talked to God several times as well. We had lost a lot of our corpsmen during the Korean War, and there were not many on active duty at this time. All the rationalizing I did during the night did nothing to clear my mind, and I truly had no idea what I would say to the major.

Around 0400, I took a long, hot shower and did some more thinking and praying. When Ryan and Reeves knocked at 0700, I immediately opened the door, fully dressed and ready to go to breakfast. "I knew you would be ready," said Ryan. "You didn't go to sleep last night, did you?"

We all laughed when I said, "What are you talking about? I slept like a baby."

We walked down the hall to John's room, and he was still in bed, sound asleep. Ryan pulled the door closed slowly, "We'll just let him get his beauty sleep."

Reeves looked around and said wryly, "It won't do any good!" We went on to the chow hall and went through the line, loading our trays with food to start the day right.

We had just finished eating when Major Gordon and Gunny Potter came in and sat down with us. Reeves went to the line and got a carafe of coffee and two more cups. "Good move, Reeves. We'll try to get you a raise for that," said the gunny.

"Thanks, Gunny, I could use another dollar a month."

The jokes stopped when the major sat his cup down and said, "We have business to discuss, but I think we had better go over to my office. We have moved all our offices and people here to Yokohama. I don't want any discussions here in public."

Here it comes. "Huh-oh," I said, "I don't like the sound of this."

Gunny laughed and said, "You don't have anything to worry about, Doc. This doesn't involve you—well, not much!" We moved on out and Reeves went by John's room to let him know where we were. I think he told him to go on to breakfast and meet us in the major's office.

The major had a large office with a conference table that would seat eight people. "I'm sure you have it figured out by now, Doc. Our recon team is going back to Sariwon in a couple weeks, and we have secured clearance for you to accompany the team as our medical support. Your ship's doctor didn't have any reservations about your physical ability to accept the assignment. The real question is how *you* feel about the mission this soon after your hospitalization."

"Before he answers, Major," interrupted Ryan, "you should know that I took it upon myself to go by Doc's room last night and discuss this possibility with him."

Gunny then said, "Don't let him take all the blame or credit, Major. I sent him and Reeves by to fill him in and give him time to mull this thing over. I'm sure you'll agree."

"That's fine, Gunny. I know how close you guys are, and I'm sure that was the right decision."

"I want to say it's still pretty much a surprise, even after thinking it over for several hours. This tells me how much confidence you have in me and makes me feel good," I said. "All I really have to do is to think back at the thanks we got from those first POWs we brought out. I just feel like I don't have any choice but to accept that I have volunteered one more time."

The major laughed and said, "Yeah, we're all volunteers! Actually, we *are* all volunteers for these missions. We all remember the looks on their faces. We're glad you will be back on our team, Doc. I do feel like it is *our* team, because I'm going to be leading this mission. Now we can get down to the business of planning the mission. You need to go back to your ship, leave all your personal gear in your locker, and just bring your shaving kit. You know the drill. You will be going back to the *Sultan* after this trip. Just be back here at 1700 hours. Dr. Secunda said none of the other corpsmen are on the ship today, so this'll be a good time for you to check out with him and not run into anyone. Reeves will give you a ride over to the docks and back."

"Sending a bodyguard to make sure I don't back out, aren't you?" I said.

"We know you are anxious to get back with the marines," the gunny said. "We can tell it's in your blood to get back on the recon team."

Reeves and I went on out front. We took a sedan back to the harbor. "I was just getting my sea legs back, and here we go again. This'll probably be my last trip since I'm getting out in September. My four years is about up," I said.

"You'll probably re-enlist, Doc. You won't know what to do with yourself as a civilian."

"No, I'm going to take my separation, but I'll be in the Navy Reserves for another four years. I want to go back to college and get my degree. Then, maybe I'll come back in as an officer."

Reeves replied, "No, you won't come back either, Doc. Once you get out, you will probably go on to finish school, but you'll get married, and when the children start coming, you won't give the military another thought."

"You think you have got me pegged, don't you? I really don't know if I would come back into the military or not. But I do want to finish college, and it probably *won't* be in the medical field. I've always wanted to get an accounting degree and some law school, but not to be a courtroom lawyer. Enough of that, none of us know what we want to do anymore!"

We arrived at the harbor, and Reeves had a pass to drive onto the docks. "The gunny got us this pass so we could drive in and take care of business more easily. Sometimes, we have gear to take back to the vehicles."

"Good idea, Reeves. Come on aboard the ship with me, and I'll show you our digs. This sure beats a foxhole anytime." We went up to the hospital first, and Dr. Secunda and Nurse Reynolds were in his office going over records.

The doctor looked up, "Come on in, Gentry. I understand you are going to take a little vacation from us. Lieutenant Reynolds knows about your status. We have been over your record, and you appear to be handling everything without any problems. I told the major that I thought you were ready to go with his team on this mission. Actually, it sounds exciting. I'd like to go with you since I always did enjoy hiking and camping."

Lieutenant Reynolds said, "Me, too."

"You should come on with us, sir," said Reeves, "we enjoy plenty of hiking and camping."

The doctor checked my blood pressure, listened to my heart, looked into my eyes and ears, and all that good stuff. "I can't think of a good reason to not approve you, Gentry. You are physically able to take on the temporary duty, and the mental part is for you to decide."

No one laughed about the mental part, so I just said, "Thanks for working with us on this, Dr. Secunda. I'll see you in a month or so when I rejoin your crew."

Reeves and I went on down to my stateroom, and he couldn't believe our quarters. "This is nicer than the Staff NCO quarters you stayed in last night. I believe I'd just stay on this ship until I retired."

I told him to come with me. "This is our dining room." When we walked in, one of the waiters stuck his head in from the galley, "Are you ready to eat now?"

I sat down and said, "Yes, Juan, I have a guest with me for lunch, if that's okay. I didn't think you would be serving in here since we are in port."

He handed us the menu and said, "It will be okay. The crew's mess hall is full now." Reeves could not believe the meal we had. "You navy guys really do have it made."

I just let him talk. This was the only duty station I'd ever seen with this many nice benefits as we had on this ship.

Back at the marine barracks, Reeves was telling everyone about the fancy cruise ship I was living on. None of them knew either that the army had any ships with civilian crews. "I have never even heard of the USS *Sultan*," said the gunny, "but I have traveled on the *Anderson* and the *Breckenridge*, and they are navy ships."

I replied, "That's right. Most of the military on the *Sultan* are short–timers, so it looks like they're just buttering us up to get us to re-enlist."

The major had Ryan take me over to get my uniforms and gear so I would be dressed like a marine again. "This'll hold you until we get to Korea," said Ryan. "We have a few days of reviewing the information we have received. Then we'll put the full team together when we get back over to Seoul. Major Gordon wants you to sit in on our meetings—I guess to keep you out of trouble. No, he wants everyone on the team in on the planning. That works better for all of us."

The following morning, the sessions started in the major's smaller conference room. "There are still a lot of questions to be answered," the major stated. "There have been some very reliable sources telling of American, British, and other POWs sighted in North Korea recently. The latest ones were seen just south of Sariwon working on the railroad. We all know about where that probably is. We've been there and are going back to hopefully get the rest of those guys out."

He turned on the overhead projector and showed us photos taken from the U-2s. Of course, we could not identify any individuals from the photos, but we could see figures along the tracks. Then he put up maps that pinpointed the area where the POWs were last seen and the camp where they were supposedly being kept. It was not the exact area we had previously raided, but it wasn't far from it.

The major and the gunny decided on a total of eleven men for this trip. If we needed more than that, they'd have several on ready, but sometimes too many men could be a hindrance instead of a help. The planning sessions continued for one more day, and the major decided we were ready to move on to Seoul and put the full team together. "That's all we can do here. Let's move on to Korea, and we'll get this show on the road sooner than expected. I'll make all the arrangements to fly out tomorrow. Be ready to leave at 0600 from the front of the barracks. Reveille will be at 0400 hours, so hit the sack early tonight. We're going to have a busy week, so you need all the rest you can get. Gunny will let you know of any changes. Dismissed!"

"Aye, aye, sir."

We headed to the barracks and started packing our duffle bags. Less than an hour later, Gunny hit the door, "Off and on, you jarheads. You've got ten minutes to get dressed and fall in out front." I thought he was going to take us on one of his surprise hikes. "Grab your bags; we're headed to Tachikawa Airbase and flying out to Seoul at 2200 hours."

Then it hit me right in the gut. This is really happening. We're going back to Korea. After a couple of minutes, I was all right with it, but it scared me for a few seconds. "You had this planned all along, didn't you, Gunny," I said.

He laughed, "No, not really. I had just gone over to the NCO Club for a beer, and evidently, Gordon knew where to find me. I didn't even get a chance to finish my mug of beer! Come on, let's go!"

We lugged our bags outside, and there was Major Gordon in the front of a small bus waiting for us. We loaded our half-full duffle bags in the back of the bus and climbed aboard. The bus pulled out and headed for Tachikawa. "Pull out your cooler, Gunny," I said.

"What cooler are you talking about?" He laughed as Reeves walked back and grabbed the cooler of beer and the bag of sandwiches and pepperoni.

"Old habits are hard to break," said Major Gordon. "This has been our send-off for the five years I've been doing this."

We enjoyed the trip to the airbase. We were talkative at first, but by the time we got there, we were all talked out and starting to think about what was ahead of us. It isn't good to think too much at times like this, even though it was a week or so away. When we got to the airbase and unloaded our gear, Gunny noted half of the cooler of beer was unopened.

"Driver, take this cooler back to the garage—and you guys enjoy it after you get off duty. There are some sandwiches left over for you also." The driver thanked him and said there were four others in his unit, and it would make a good midnight snack for them.

The plane was already warming up for us. We got there just before 2200, so they were ready to go. All our gear was loaded, and we were soon strapped in to the real, cushioned seats. We didn't have to put up with the canvas seats this time, either. The crew chief closed the door to the C-47, and we taxied across the tarmac to the end of the runway. The pilot swung the plane around, revved the engines, and away we went. The plane roared down the runway, and as soon as we lifted off, he veered off to the left and up at a steeper climb than we were used to.

"We've got a real hot dog of a pilot up there!" said the major. "He must be in a hurry or is trying to impress us marines with his flying skills. I don't know which it is."

Everyone laughed and the crew chief spoke up, "That's just the way he flies. He used to fly fighter planes, and I told him one day he couldn't tell a C-47 from a P-51."

The major reached out and shook the crew chief's hand, saying, "Sergeant, I like the way you talk and see things. We need to get you on our team."

The sergeant looked around and asked, "What kind of team do you have, Major?"

Corporal Reeves said, "We're a subsidiary of the Harlem Globetrotters, but we're traveling in disguise to confuse the North Koreans."

Everyone laughed like crazy and probably would have fallen out of our seats if we weren't strapped in. "You could have fooled me," said the crew chief, "and I won't ask any more questions, because I can see already what kind of answers you are going to give me. I hope you enjoy your flight." He turned and headed toward the cockpit, and we knew he was going to tell the pilot that he was carrying the Harlem Globetrotters in disguise.

The pilot did walk back through to the back of the plane but only said, "Hello, how are you doing?" or something like that.

When he came back through, the major spoke to him, "Hey, Captain, did you find a basketball hoop back there somewhere?" Everyone roared with laughter and the captain just looked around at us, shook his head, and headed back to the cockpit.

We landed near Seoul where there was a bus waiting for us, as expected. It was after midnight, and we were taken directly to the barracks. "Hit the sack, men," said the major. "You can sleep in until 0600. I don't want you to get too soft with this easy living. We'll fall in at 0620 and go to breakfast together. As you remember, we'll go everywhere together for a while."

That 0600 reveille came awfully fast. We bounced up, secured our gear, and were out front by 0620. The major was waiting for us with the six other members of our team. There were Lance Corporals Earnest Edwards and John Grayson, Private Jackson Holder, Sergeant Kwan, and Private Rho, all of whom I knew from previous trips. There was one new member, Private Robert Duncan; this was his first mission. We shook hands all around and fell in on the street two by two.

After a good breakfast, we went back to the barracks for thirty minutes, and then the major took us to a conference room in the building next door. He went over all the photos and maps to bring everyone up to date. "We don't know for certain that the men spotted working on the railroad are POWs, but our best-educated opinion is that there are more American, British, Australian, South Korean, and maybe other prisoners being held by the North Koreans—or maybe in China by now. It is our duty to find any of those men—and women if there are any—and bring them back to freedom. Now, here are our plans on how we'll go about this."

The brainstorming went on for two more days with input from a couple experts and a former POW who had been there. Then the major turned us over to the gunny for some physical torture—sorry, I meant physical training—and then a day on the rifle range. The major started his meeting with the brass to arrange the technicals and logistics of our mission.

Gunny started the next morning with a five-mile run at 0500 hours. That sure did make breakfast taste good—especially the cold orange juice. They always made sure we ate plenty of fruit and juices when we were in training. The gunny took us—that is, ran us—over to the obstacle course and went over the procedures for rappelling from helicopters. They had twenty-foot ropes installed for us to climb and then rappel back down. After two or three climbs, it's a *helluva* lot easier to rappel than it is to climb. We ran obstacle courses for two hours before we took a break for lunch. We feasted on rations just as if we were out on a mission.

"That's enough lying around. Off and on. Put on these fifteen-pound packs we have rigged for you, and let's go for a walk." Each of us, including the gunny, strapped on the backpacks, and off we went. No one asked where or how far we were going. We figured we could walk anywhere the gunny walked. Truth be known, he could probably out-walk everyone of us. It felt like there were rocks in the backpacks.

We just kept them pulled tight, so they wouldn't bounce against our backs.

The walk lasted for two hours with only one water break. When we returned to the obstacle course, Gunny said, "Take those packs off and stow 'em in the shed over there, and fall back in on the street. We've got one more place I want you to go."

The team fell in on the street, and Gunny bellowed, "About face! Now double time—all the way back to the barracks! That's all for today." That last half mile was the easiest exercise of the day. He went into the barracks with us. "Okay, get your showers and be ready to go to the chow hall at 1700 hours. It was a pretty good day. We'll try to do it all right tomorrow!"

The next day was pretty much the same. Then on the third day, we went to the rifle range. We all fired .45 caliber M1911 pistols, M-1 Garands, M-1 carbines, 03 sniper rifles, 12-gauge shotguns, and then each got to throw five hand grenades. A couple of guys fired the Garands with grenade launchers. This is one day we all enjoyed, but it was about as tiring as running the obstacle course.

At 0800 the fourth day, we were taken to Major Gordon's conference room. "Later today, we'll move up to the Munsan Airstrip. We'll start the tactical training there and get down to brass tacks. We're about ready to go get this thing done. Go get all your gear and fall out in front of the barracks at 0915 hours. The bus will be there to take us on up to Munsan. Dismissed."

"Aye, aye, sir!"

The bus was loaded and we were moving on north out of Seoul at 0915. We were all ready to get going. "There's no beer cooler and sandwiches on this bus, just to let you know. Your weapons, ammo, and other gear will be issued at Munsan. We have everything ready for us up there. Doc, you know where to pick up your medical packs when we get there. Take care of that first."

I acknowledged "Yes, sir. I'll go see Corpsman Young when we get there."

It was a slow, bumpy ride up to Munsan. The road did not seem to be in as good condition as it was last trip. But, we made it in three hours after stopping once for a roadside break. We arrived at our tents at the airfield. There was an officer's car waiting when we got there. After we'd climbed down from the bus and were walking around to get our gear, the car door opened and out stepped USMC General Billings and General Starky.

"Attention on deck!"

We popped to attention, and the major saluted the generals. General Billings saluted back and said, "At ease, men. We just got back from a helicopter tour of the border and were told you and your men were here, Major Gordon. I want to congratulate you men on your past missions, and as I've said before, the public is just as grateful, even though they don't know all the details—and probably won't. By the way, Major, I saw your father in Manila last week, and he is well. He seems to be enjoying his new command. You men have a good leader here in Major Gordon. I have known his family for years. Carry on."

The generals got back into their sedan and were gone, but everyone's eyes were still on Major Gordon. "Okay, get your gear and stow it in your tents. The corporal over here will show you where to go."

No one said anything, but questions had been asked as to how Gordon had gone from first lieutenant to captain and then to major in a little over two years. We still didn't know the answers, just more questions. I didn't say anything, but I do remember an Admiral Gordon on the *Anderson* several months ago traveling from Hawaii to the Philippines. I never saw him but a couple times, so I didn't know enough about him to say anything.

Reveille came at 0600, and the gunny called us out for another five-mile run. We all fell in, and Major Gordon fell in at the back of the line. "Lead us out, Gunny," he said.

"Let's start out slow, men. I'll set the pace. Forward ... H*UT*!" Gunny led us on the jog at varying paces for the full five miles. Then all eleven of us ate at the chow hall. Afterwards, we went out into the field and went through several exercises. This was the routine for three days. The major took part in all activities, leading some of them, just like Lieutenant Skinner used to do.

During the second day, the major sent me to get my medical bags and gear. Young had been transferred out, and I didn't get to see him this time, but I got everything I needed and then some. They said Young was transferred to Pearl Harbor. Wouldn't you know it; where else would Lanny go?

The fourth day, the major called us together when we fell in at 0600. "There won't be any more training today. As a matter of fact, that truck over there holds your weapons, ammo, rations, and other supplies. We're flying north just after midnight tonight, probably at 0100 hours. You'll be issued your gear and supplies, and we'll have one more skull session at 1000 and another at 1300, before we take a rest break. You'll check out all your weapons at 1600 hours at the little firing range just past the airstrip over there. We'll have another session after we eat this evening to get our final assignments. Come on over and check out your weapons and ammo. The time is here—time to return to Sariwon."

The sergeant checked our names off the clipboard as we picked up our respective weapons, ammunition, and other hardware.

Chapter 8

Return to Sariwon

The evening passed slowly while we were preparing for the mission back to Sariwon, and the search for the POWs. There were two ammunition depots and apparent anti-aircraft–gun emplacements that were spotted on the U-2 photos. We were going to have a full plate on this trip. I started my double check with everyone to make sure they each had their individual first-aid kits on their belts. Then I made sure they all had at least three spare pairs of socks and their foot powder—of course. By then, it was 2100, and everyone was trying to lie down and get some rest before we had to leave.

Major Gordon came to the openings between the two tents, so he could talk to all of us at the same time. "We'll be pulling out at 0230 hours, so you'll assemble outside the tents at 0200. If there are no questions, get some rest, and we'll see you then." No one had anything to say, we had not been this quiet in a long time. It was time to rest, think, and to pray … and maybe not in that order.

At 0200, Gunny called us out with all our weapons and gear. "Fall in outside your tents. Check all your weapons and make sure your gear is secure. We'll be taking three helicopters tonight. Here are your assignments: number one will carry Major Gordon, Corporal Reeves, Private Holder, and Doc Gentry; number two will be Lance Corporal Edwards, Private Duncan, Private Rho, and me; and in number three, we have Sergeant Ryan, Lance Corporal Grayson, Sergeant Kwan—plus, you'll carry the explosives and supplies. When we reach the objective, we'll land in the order of our numbers. We don't know yet if we'll be able to set down or rappel, just wait for our orders from the pilot."

"All right men," said the major as he started walking toward the helicopters. "Come on, it's time to go. You'll note the birds are painted to look like North Korean helicopters. Okay, climb aboard your assigned 'copter and settle in." Everyone sat back and waited as the motors started and revved up. until we soon lifted off and were on our way. The major told us, "As before, we can no longer fly straight north over the border, so we'll fly west over the Yellow Sea and then north over Korea Bay. After that, we'll come back inland as low as possible to avoid detection to within five miles of our objective, if possible."

We were flying very low over the water. At one point, we went close by a fishing boat and his mast went right beside us. That was too low it seemed to me. After forty minutes or so, we started turning to the right ever so slightly. We pulled up to a couple hundred feet, and the pilot said to us over the intercom, "There's a couple patrol boats down there, and we didn't want them to get too close a look at us." He swung the helicopter back and forth a couple times as a way to say hello to the patrol boats. Then we dropped down below fifty feet to stay under their radar. Believe it or not, I dropped off to sleep for a short while, and when I looked out, we were zigzagging over land.

"Check your gear and get ready," came over the speaker. "You have about ten minutes to your destination. Stand by."

The major said, "We still don't know if we'll be able to set down or not. Be ready for anything." We soon started slowing down and circling an opening. We could see it was very rocky with thick underbrush, so we were going to have to rappel. We deployed the ropes and were standing by.

"Get ready, Major; you'll have to rappel. Sorry about that; just be careful. Okay, get ready ... three ... two ... one—GO, GO, GO ...!"

Holder was out first. I followed him down the rope, and when I hit the ground, I jumped back, and Reeves came down with the BAR on a rope, which he grabbed as he landed. Then, here came Major Gordon. We all dropped about five feet apart, and the helicopter circled out and then number two came in, followed a minute later by number three, which had to come in a little lower to get Ryan's baggage off. They sure didn't want to drop it very far with the amount of explosives he was carrying. In less than two minutes, the three helicopters dropped their cargo and flew out of sight on their way back west toward the coast.

"This way to the tree line," said the major. "We have to get out of the middle of this open field. Gunny, count 'em off to make sure we didn't lose one back there."

The gunny responded, "All eleven accounted for. Ryan, Grayson, and Kwan are bringing up the rear with the extra baggage." We made it into the trees and everyone sat down and listened to the sounds of the night for a few minutes. There were no unusual sounds that I could hear, not even the helicopters.

The major went over to Private Rho, "According to the pilot's last reading, we're five miles from our objective. How does that sound to you?" Rho stood up and said, "That sounds about right, sir." He shone his small light on a red spot on the map." This is our location on this map. We can head northeast from here and should be at our next checkpoint well before daylight. Sergeant Kwan and I are very familiar with this part of the country."

I went around to each man and made sure there were no injuries. "Everyone's okay and ready to go, Major," I said as I got around to his position.

The major called Gunny and Ryan over. "Get 'em loaded up and let's get moving."

Ryan distributed his load around to everyone that could carry a little more weight. He carried the heaviest part, and he kept all the fuses isolated. He didn't give me any because of the medical bags I had strapped to my back and belt.

Edwards and Rho took point, and Holder and Duncan brought up the rear as we started east down the mountain. Kwan and Gordon had a conversation going on about our first contact. Kwan and Rho both knew the person, so that was good. It took us a half hour to get down to the valley, which we would follow for a couple miles before starting back up another hilly section.

"Take cover!" said Edwards. We dropped down behind the underbrush.

"What is it, Edwards?"

He was standing hunched over and said, "There are what look like a pair of headlights on the other side of the valley at about three o'clock. I can't hear them yet, but they're on the move."

We all took a peek over the bushes and we could see the lights. "There are some more coming behind it," said Kwan. "There is a road over there, but it will head away from us after they make the next turn.

That is the road to Pengstan, which is southeast of Sariwon. We can go now."

"Move out, men," said Gordon. "And good job Edwards. You've got a sharp eye."

We picked up our step so we could get on out of the valley. It felt like we were more vulnerable than when we were in the mountains, although it was much easier walking. Before long, we got to the first hills and started the climb. We kept up the pace for a while, until Gunny called for a water break. "It's a little more tiring when we've got all this extra weight hanging on us. Now you see why I refuse to gain weight, it's too hard to carry around!"

In another ninety minutes, we came to the top of a small hill and Kwan said, "This is our checkpoint, Major. You can see the railroad about a half mile straight ahead. Keep the men here, and I will go meet with our first contact." He dropped his backpack and left his rifle there. "Good luck, Kwan," said the major. Kwan was soon out of sight down the hill.

Gunny Potter put Duncan, Holder, and Grayson on first watch; spread out around the perimeter of our little encampment. "Now's a good time to eat your rations," he said. "Go slow on your water until we can refill our canteens. Remember, no fire and no smokes. Everyone keep your eyes open." We spread out and found a place to sit and eat our rations. Not real tasty, but they did fill us up for a while. I stretched out for a few minutes and was asleep in no time.

Someone was shaking my shoulder, waking me quickly. It was Reeves. "We had to wake you up, Doc. We couldn't tell if you were calling ducks or trying to start an earthquake." They all laughed as quietly as they could. I must have really been sawing logs in my sleep.

"Two figures are coming up the hill," said Grayson. "There's one flash of light."

Gunny replied, "Give them two flashes back and be alert."

Then Grayson said, "They came back with three flashes. It's them, but we'll keep our eyes open."

Sergeant Kwan and another Korean came in and sat down next to the major and Gunny. Kwan introduced the contact to them, and Major Gordon asked him about any POWs in the area and where they were being held.

The contact, a Mr. Huang, replied in broken English, "The prisoners were taken away on a train going north toward Pyongyang two days back. I have seen none since then. I saw eleven prisoners two weeks ago, and five were taken by train last week. The other six were taken away this week. I am so sorry."

The major replied, "It is no fault of your own. You've done us a great service by coming to our aid with this information on this day. Thank you, Mr. Huang." Then Major Gordon surprised everyone when he talked with Mr. Huang in Korean. None of us knew what they were saying, but Kwan and Rho sat down with a chuckle.

Mr. Huang answered, "You are very welcome, Mr. Major. If you will bring your men with me now; I have a place to conceal your men that cannot be seen from the air. This is not a good place."

Sergeant Kwan added, "He's right, Major, there's a lot of helicopter and airplane traffic in this area since we were here before."

"Okay, men" he replied, "Let's get down off this hill before the sun comes up. Grab all your gear and let's move out."

Mr. Huang and Sergeant Kwan led us down to the bottom of the hill and then off to the left. We walked about a half mile to a cave hidden back in the trees. "You'll be safe here for as long as you need to stay. Mr. Kwan knows where my home is just five minutes away. There are two openings to the cave that will give you a good view of the valley. I will go now and will return before the sun sets in the evening."

"Thank you again," said the major, "We'll not leave our cover in the daylight unless absolutely necessary."

Mr. Huang showed us through the cave and lit a torch for us. He then left us as the sun was beginning to light up the sky. "I'm glad we have this place of concealment, but am very disappointed about the prisoners being moved before we got here," said the gunny.

"All is not lost," said Kwan. "According to Mr. Huang, there is one weapons and storage depot five miles to the south of us and another ten miles southwest of that one. They are within our range."

The major replied, "That's true. Mr. Huang told me about those, and when I asked him about the anti-aircraft guns, he said he did not know about them. I showed him the suspected locations on the map, and he said he would find out what he could today."

Holder, Grayson and Duncan now had a chance to eat. Gunny put Edwards on watch at the mouth of the cave and put me at the back opening while the others got some rest. Gordon, Potter, and Ryan moved outside the cave and hid in the trees overlooking the valley. There was an excellent view of the railroad, several buildings, and homes scattered all around the area. None of the buildings that we could see near the railroad were fenced in and nothing looked like barracks or a military facility.

"I don't know if we're at the right location or not," I heard Ryan say.

"This is the right place," said the major, "It checks out with the map and photos. We just got here too late. We'll make some more inquires before we go after the ammo depots. It's imperative that we find those poor lost men if at all possible. They think the whole world's forgotten them, and sometimes it appears that's the case. We're not going to give up that easy."

Then Potter asked, "Why don't we let Kwan and Rho go out and question some of the people they know? Maybe they can find out more than Huang can by himself."

"That may be a possibility, Gunny, but we'd better discuss it with Huang first and see what he finds out. I don't want to get too many out there asking questions."

Then I heard engine noises and spotted vehicles coming through the underbrush. "Major Gordon, there are three jeeps and a truck coming through the underbrush in this direction."

He answered back "I see 'em, Doc. Alert everyone and have Reeves bring his BAR out here. Doc, go get the 03 for Ryan and have the others stay in the cave for now." I did as he said and then he sent me back inside the cave. Everyone else crowded around the mouth and tried to see through the leaves.

The jeeps and truck came within fifty yards of our location and kept going on up the valley. "Kwan," called Gordon, "take Grayson with you to see if they stopped at Huang's house or if they kept going."

Kwan came running by, "I was about to go check on that. I will go alone. It will be faster and safer that way."

Kwan came back in fifteen minutes with Mr. Huang. "They did not stop, but they may be back later in the morning," said Huang. "They have stopped before and asked me questions about different locations between here and Pyongyang. They know I was a construction engineer when this section of the railroad was built. Do not worry, I will certainly not let them know of your presence. They pass by here every two days."

The major said, "That is interesting, Huang, how many men are there in the jeeps and the truck?"

"It appeared there are two men in each jeep, two men in the front of the truck, and I did not see anyone in the back of the truck. They are maybe going to get supplies for their camp. It did not appear to be a search party." The major thanked Huang in his language and sent him back to his home.

"What the hell are you up to, Major?" asked the gunny. "That didn't sound like an idle question. Are we going to get us some vehicles?"

The major laughed, "We've been around each other too long, Potter. You know we have to ambush them when they come back through and see what kind of supplies they have. Then we'll do a little hit-and run-operation on the ammunition depots. With a little luck, we'll also find those gun emplacements."

Ryan looked at them. "I've always thought both of you were crazy. and I know it now. So, how are we going to pull this off?"

Major Gordon laughed and said, "This will take a little reminiscing on Gunny's part, but we have what it takes, and the Koreans will think their own men did it."

Gunny laughed, "I knew what you were going to come up with, Major. This will be a breeze, especially if they don't have a dozen men in the back of the truck."

Major Gordon assembled the team in the cave and told us he had a plan, or rather Gunny Potter had a plan. Gunny stood up, "A few years back, our platoon was bogged down over in Sin'gye, and the North Koreans had some reinforcements coming in behind us. Anyway, we ambushed two trucks, killing the soldiers, and put on their uniforms. We then drove the trucks into the middle of the other North Korean soldiers with our men hidden in the back. Our men opened fire on them and got us out of a messy situation."

Grayson said, "Yeah, a regular Trojan Horse trick. It's worked before, so it'll probably work again."

The major laid out his idea of concealing men on each side of the path the trucks took and then having Kwan and Rho act as decoys to get them to stop. We would have to put a lookout up the way to let us know when the vehicles were returning.

"Before we do anything else, I need to explain something to those of you who haven't known me as long as the others. I was raised in a military family that dates back many generations. My father is Admiral Gordon, that General Billings mentioned in front of all of you a few days ago who has a command in the Pacific. They went to the naval academy together and have been close friends ever since. I also went to the naval academy and chose the marine corps since my father was in the navy. I've never used his influence to gain a promotion or any special treatment. My promotions have come faster than most, but I've worked for every one of them. Maybe I've been at the right place at the right time. I'm only telling you about this because you're the closest family I have. Now, none of this will ever be mentioned again in any conversation—*period*."

Then the major said, "Down to business. We'll try to capture those soldiers alive if possible. Kwan—you and Rho devise a plan to get 'em to stop so we can surround the vehicles and not have to shoot anyone. Maybe we can get some information from the soldiers concerning the prisoners. Rho—you and Reeves go find a location where you can spot the vehicles approaching and still have time to alert us. Holder, you go with them to their observation point and then return to let us know where they are located."

The three moved out to establish their observation post. The major sat down with Potter and Ryan to finalize their plan and our assignments to capture the Korean vehicles. Then the major and the other two got up, saying, "Kwan, come on with us, and we'll scout the area to find a suitable ambush site. All you men check your weapons and get ready to go. Just rest and be alert at the same time.

All the men found places to relax outside the cave under the trees. It was much more comfortable than the damp floor in the cavern. While we were waiting, Ryan gave us all our ambush assignments and reviewed them once again to answer any questions.

"They're in sight about three or four miles up the valley," shouted Reeves and Rho as they came running.

"Follow me," said Major Gordon. We all ran out through the trees into the open to our designated places behind boulders and in the underbrush on either side of the pathway.

Kwan and Rho, who had put on North Korean soldier uniforms supplied by Huang, were sitting on a large wooden box, also from Huang, in the middle of the path where we expected the small convoy to travel. As they approached, our decoys stood up and waved their arms for them to stop. They were yelling to them in Korean to stop and help them with their box. I didn't think they would stop, but the vehicles slowly came to a stop with all of them yelling back and forth. Kwan jumped up with both arms in the air, "Now, Major."

We jumped up pointing our rifles at the shocked soldiers. We caught them completely by surprise and not a shot was fired. Reeves had been positioned to cover the rear of the truck with his BAR just in case there were more soldiers riding in the back.

We dragged the soldiers out onto the ground. We took their weapons and searched them as they spread out on the ground. There were eight uniformed North Korean soldiers; two of them were apparently officers. The three jeeps had extra weapons and ammunition in the rear seat compartments. The truck was loaded with dynamite, tools for working on the tracks, a few cross ties, spikes, steel plates, and several cases of food supplies. There were also four five-gallon cans of gasoline.

"Don't take them anywhere near our camp. We want to keep that a secret from them. Tie them all to trees over here out of sight," said Gordon. "Pull the truck and jeeps over through the trees so they cannot be seen from the air." I got into one of the jeeps to move it; the engine was still running. We moved them and checked to see what other kinds of contraband we had captured.

In the meantime, Major Gordon, Kwan, and Edwards took the two North Korean officers away from the enlisted men to question them out of their earshot. Rho sat down with the enlisted soldiers and started talking with them nonchalantly. I don't know what he was saying, but they were talking to each other before long. After a half hour, Rho came over to us and said, "the prisoners we are looking for were taken up north to do some work in Pyongyang for a month or more. They say there's no other American prisoners around that they know about. I need to tell the major what I have just learned from them." Rho walked over to the major and was gone for a good while.

Private Holder said, "Whoa, look what I have found," as he walked over to one of the captives and pulled a knife from one of their boots. "I just saw it when he straightened his leg out."

Grayson came over, "I thought they had been searched better than that. Pull their boots off and search them again." We checked all of them and that apparently was the only weapon overlooked.

Gordon came back with the others and had the officers tied to trees with the other North Koreans. Holder and Duncan were left to guard them. The major called us all aside and said, "We got very nearly the same story from both the officers and the enlisteds by the time we were through. The people we want to find seem to be completely out of this territory, and we don't stand a prayer going after them in Pyongyang. We're left with the rest of our agenda to take care of.

"I've given some thought to what to do with the prisoners. It'll make more sense to turn these captives over to Huang's associates. We'll keep the vehicles for our use to make a quick strike on the two ammo depot objectives." Potter and Ryan agreed with the major; so that made it unanimous as far as we were concerned.

For the third time during the day, we heard some helicopters flying over the valley and across the mountains. They didn't appear to be coming anywhere near us. Kwan had gone to find Mr. Huang and fill him in on our status quo. While we were taking a rest break, Huang and three others came in with Kwan. Major Gordon talked with the men and explained what we had done. Huang asked us to unload the supplies from the truck that we did not need, and his people would take care of them.

Then Mr. Huang and his men selected several weapons and all the ammo they could carry. We got all eight prisoners onto their feet, tied their hands behind their backs, and secured them all together with a rope so one could not easily run away. Huang led them away with his men covering them from behind. They turned to the right, away from the direction of Huang's home and were soon out of site.

"Okay, Gunny, it's now 1600, and we need four hours' rest after this busy day. We'll get some sleep and get back to work at 2000. I'll have a plan for us by then. This will be different than anything we've tried yet. Set two men on a two-hour watch rotation. Go get some sleep, you guys, if you can. We're going to have a busy night." We were all ready to lie down for a while, regardless how fast our adrenaline was pumping. It didn't take long for us to drift off to sleep after we did sprawl out and relax.

At 1800 hours, Reeves awakened me to go on watch. We went out and sent Duncan and Holder back inside to catch a little sleep. Major Gordon and Sergeant Ryan were sitting by the wall of the cave making notes by the light of a lantern. I took a position against a tree by the mouth of the cave, and Reeves took the back entrance. It was beginning to get dark, and I could see lights coming on in the shacks across the valley. None of the lights were moving; so that was good. I could hear an airplane in the distance. Then we heard a train coming from the north. It was not moving very fast, and it went on south out of sight, but I could hear the steam engine puffing along for a good while. After that, all I could hear were the natural sounds of the night. The birds were quiet, but the crickets and something like a whippoorwill were all the sounds right now.

The two-hour watch went quietly, and at 2000, I went in to awaken Major Gordon and the others. "Hey, Doc, it's time to hold reveille on these sleepy heads," said the major. "I was just getting ready to come out and check on you guys." He turned up the lantern and lit another torch from the one already burning on the front wall. "Up and at 'em, you lazy bums!" he shouted. "We've got a full night's work ahead of us. Let's go make some noise! Gunny, Ryan, and I have worked out a plan to take care of the ammo depots in a rather quick order. There are not supposed to be any military facilities within a hundred miles of the DMZ, so we have to keep them in compliance.

"There are no clouds tonight so we will be able to travel most of the way without lights, which should help. We will go with two men in the jeeps and the remainder in the truck. All the cargo except the dynamite was removed from the truck for Huang and his people. We have enough explosives now to rig a jeep to run into each of the depots if the situation is right. First, we have to get there, so let's load up and get moving."

We got all our gear loaded and started the drive on south toward our first objective. Kwan and Rho were driving the first two jeeps since they knew the roads and where the objectives were located. Gordon was with Kwan, Potter with Rho, and Ryan driving with Reeves carrying his BAR in the third jeep. Grayson was behind the wheel of the truck with Edwards riding shotgun, and the rest of us in the back. This was a little rough riding, but it sure beat walking. We moved along slowly and carefully. In about thirty minutes, Kwan led us off the road into the shadows of some trees. "We are within one hundred yards of the depot," said Kwan as we walked up to the lead jeep.

"Ryan, you take Kwan, Rho, and Edwards to take a look at our target," said the major. "If they have a fence, get the gate open so we can run a jeep through it. Check out what they've got, but don't linger too long—but you know the drill. Reeves, Grayson, and Holder will back you up outside the fence. The rest of us will stay with the vehicles. We'll look for you back here within forty minutes." They moved on out through the shadows. There were no lights visible through the trees, so we didn't know what to expect.

I was sitting on the top of the truck peering through the darkness. The quarter moon didn't put out much light, which may have been a good thing. The binoculars didn't do much good from where we were. "Major, we may need to send a couple more up there," said Gunny after about twenty minutes. "Something just doesn't feel right about this whole thing."

The major said, "I get the same feeling, Gunny. Come on, the four of us will walk a little way. Spread out and go slow so we don't spook our men."

We didn't walk but about fifty yards when we saw our men coming toward us. We signaled and met each other. Ryan said, "You've never seen anything like this. First of all, we saw no one on duty, and there are no lights on the outside. There are five buildings, including what appears to be two barracks. There's an office building and two buildings that contain explosives, ammunition, grenades, mortar shells, and cannon shells for the damned big tank sitting behind the second building. There are two jeeps and three trucks, and there's no fence around the compound. Best of all, there are about twenty barrels of gasoline stacked between the two storage buildings. We opened one barrel and turned it over, spilling the gas to make it interesting."

"Did you say *tank*, and did you see any lights in the barracks or other buildings?" Gunny asked.

"I didn't see any lights," answered Kwan, "but I did go near the door of one building and heard some talking and laughing. They were talking about their last party, so at least two of them are awake, and yes, there was a Russian tank behind the buildings."

"Ryan, go rig up a jeep with explosives on the front like you told us. We'll light a sixty-second fuse on it and roll it into the barrels. Have the other vehicles ready, and we'll be out of here. You said you had done another one like this not long ago, so it should be easy this time," said the major.

Ryan said, "Yeah, Gunny and I rigged vehicles that way three times about two years back. Gunny, if you and Reeves will help me with this jeep, the rest of you guys can get your gear ready to go. I'll set a second fuse at seventy seconds just to be sure." We all got busy stowing our gear in the two jeeps and truck and were ready to go by the time Ryan had worked his magic.

All the vehicles were rigged, loaded, and ready to go. We started the engines as quietly as we could. Ryan got in the rigged jeep and slowly pulled out. We followed behind, and as we approached the compound, we turned to the right onto the road to our next objective. Ryan stopped his jeep, tied the steering wheel in place, and got out. He and Gunny lit the two fuses and then slid the jeep into low gear moving toward the barrels.

"That's going straight as an arrow. Let's go, Gunny," Ryan said out loud and ran to the truck as the jeeps were already moving up the hill. We pulled them up into the bed of the truck as we drove away.

Looking back as we were driving up the little hill, we saw flames break out when the jeep hit the barrels. All of a sudden, the spilled gasoline was blazing higher than the buildings. Then the dynamite exploded and all hell broke loose. Something big exploded in the middle of the compound, and everything was on fire. We don't know what the big explosion was, but we didn't go back to see. All the buildings were ablaze, and we could hear the ammunition and shells exploding as we drove out of sight.

In a few minutes, we approached the second depot and could see the lights through the trees. Major Gordon had us pull off into a wooded area where we could not be seen from the road. "Keep the engines idling and be ready to move if necessary. Ryan, take your group up and take a look at what we have here. The rest of us will back you up. I want one driver to stay with each vehicle. Keep your eyes open and stay alert. Move out."

Edwards, Grayson, and I stayed with the vehicles. I chose the truck because it was higher and I had better vision from there. The binoculars worked a little better from this location. It was after midnight by now, and the moon seemed a little brighter. I could occasionally see the silhouettes of our men against the lights from the depot as they worked their way through the trees.

The team made their way back to our location after forty-five minutes. It was now 0100, and hopefully, the guards were all asleep. "The compound is fenced in, and we spotted two guards walking inside the gate," said Ryan. "There appears to be only one barracks here and two storage buildings. There is one open shed between the buildings where I counted about forty barrels of gasoline. We couldn't get in to check for explosives, but I made my way all around the compound and spotted one jeep and two trucks."

The major replied, "Good job, Ryan. That confirms pretty much what I saw from my vantage point in the trees. We'll handle this one about the same way, except we'll have to get the guards to open the gate. Go ahead and rig the explosives on the front of the jeep as before.

Kwan and Rho, you will drive the jeep up to the gate and persuade the guards to open the gate. Then we'll take them out, light the fuse, and run the jeep into the barrels on a short fuse. We probably won't have as much time on this one.

"Edwards and Grayson—mount your grenade launchers on the Garands and put two or three grenades through the windows of the barracks as soon as the shooting starts. Reeves, get into position to cover the barracks with the BAR. The rest of us will spread out to cover the whole compound the best we can. As soon as the charge goes off, that's the signal to make it back here to the vehicles. We'll leave the jeep here, and all of us'll go in the truck together. Holder, you're the mechanic; disable that third jeep so no one can use it to follow us. Check your weapons, put your gear in the back of the truck, and we'll move as soon as Ryan has the charge set. Be ready to light the fuses as soon as the gate is open."

Holder opened the hood and pulled the wires and cut them with his bayonet. He removed the rotor and tossed it up into the woods. "That should stop them for a while," he said as he bent down and punctured the tires. "I've got two charges set on the front bumper, so we will have two fuses to light, but that won't be a problem," said Ryan.

"Okay, men," said Gunny. "Edwards, Grayson, and Reeves—move on up into position to cover your assignments. Kwan and Rho—get the jeep back on the road and pull on up to the gate and start your charade. The rest of us will spread out and back you up. Holder, you stay in the truck, and when the shooting starts, bring the truck up on the road where we can make a quick getaway. Is everyone ready? Okay, men—move out."

The jeep pulled up to the gate, and we heard what sounded like a friendly greeting from Kwan and Rho and an answer back just as friendly. The two guards slung their rifles onto their shoulders and went to the gate. As they swung the gates open, Kwan and Rho stood up and shot the guards with their pistols. Then we heard the Garands shoot the grenades and the BAR opened up. Ryan and Gunny ran up and lit the two fuses. Kwan put the jeep in low gear, secured the steering wheel to the seat, and started it toward the shed. The rest of us were shooting into the barracks. Reeves raked the barracks with the BAR again as two more grenades were shot through the windows.

We all turned and ran back to the road and were climbing into the truck when the charges went off. The explosion ripped into the barrels of gasoline, and a wall of flame reached into the sky. Holder drove on down the road while Gunny was getting a count to be sure we were all on board. "Eleven present and accounted for," Gunny yelled through the window to the major in the front seat.

"Thanks, Gunny, and great job, men. Holder, stop the truck for a minute and let's see what we've accomplished." He slowed and stopped about a quarter mile down the road from the roaring fire. Then the explosions began. The small-arms ammo was popping, and larger shells were shooting up into the air. Then there was a huge explosion just like at the first depot. "I don't know what that was," said Ryan, "but that was large. The only thing that comes to mind is a huge pile of dynamite. Whatever it is, it finished the job. Those shells popping up into the air and exploding look like anti-aircraft shells to me. By the way, I never saw anyone come out of the barracks."

"Yes, some did come out, but they did not get far. I only saw one get off a shot, but we got them before they got to us," said Reeves.

"We were fortunate on these two dumps, and you can really call them dumps now," said the major. "Kwan, where do we go from here?"

Kwan answered, "We need to go straight ahead about three miles and turn to the right, then northwest toward Nampo or Songnim, where we can catch a ride on a fishing boat. You had better let me drive, with Rho in the front seat with me, because we will pass close to a military post as we drive toward Chaeryong. That is the road where the anti-aircraft guns were spotted on the photographs."

Holder and Major Gordon got into the back, and the two South Koreans took over as driver and shotgun. "We'd better get moving," said Gunny, "before someone comes to see what the fire is all about. Turn the headlights on so we can see where we're going. They probably know we are here by now."

Before we had gone one hundred yards, we met two jeeps with four men in each, and they stopped with one officer getting out and holding up his hand for us to stop. Kwan pulled up beside him. Then Reeves, Edwards, and Grayson jumped up from the back of the truck and started firing. In less than ten seconds, they were all down, and Kwan started on down the road. We took a right turn on the next road, driving as fast as we dared for safety's sake.

Duncan tugged at my arm and said, "Doc, take a look at my left arm. What is wrong with it?

I shined my flashlight on his arm, and it was a bloody mess. "You've been shot, Private," I said and reached for my medical bag. I handed the light to Holder, "Hold the light for me. I need another light here while I patch up Duncan. I placed a pressure bandage on his arm for a few minutes and cleaned the wound. It was basically a flesh wound, in one side and out the other; the bullet did not appear to have hit the bone. I treated and dressed the wound. He said he didn't want a morphine shot. I gave him a couple APC pills and assured him, "That should hold you until we get to an aid station."

Duncan laughed, "I didn't know I had been shot until you told me. I didn't know what hit me. I thought someone just bumped my arm."

Kwan pointed to several lights off to the left. "That's the military post I mentioned. It wasn't very large the last time I was through here. They are about one half mile off the road. It's three miles from here to the next objective." The major replied, "Everything looks good so far; so keep it moving unless something pops up."

At the three-mile mark, we pulled off onto a little side road and hid in behind the trees. "We need to go check those gun sites. There are five wood stacks just like they use as a disguise in the pictures, so let's see what they are hiding."

Ryan stood up, "Reeves and I are familiar with these things. We'll go take a look. Rho, how about you coming with us in case we run into a language barrier?"

"Sounds good, Sarge," said the major. "The rest of us will back you up from the tree line. Signal us if there's anything we need to see." The three men moved to the opening, paused, and then walked cautiously over to the stacks. Ryan walked around them one at a time, getting down on his knees and pulling out several logs. After ten minutes of prodding and pulling, they came back over to our location laughing. "They set us up on that one. There's nothing hidden there. Those are just stacks of logs made to look like the fake covers. This is the second time in the last six months I've seen this. Let's go home."

Major Gordon didn't laugh at this one. "It looks like someone is wasting our time and putting our recon team in jeopardy for nothing. I don't like this."

Reeves spoke up, "Sir, I've seen several of these sites, and when we got here, I thought we had anti-craft gun wells like we've blown up before. They looked like the real thing. They know what they're doing."

The gunny chimed in, "That's right, Major. These were probably set up as a trap to catch us here trying to destroy them. Let's get out of here and find a fishing boat and head for a cold beer and a hot steak."

"You're right, of course, Gunny," said the major. "Let's get back to the truck and get out of this God forsaken place. It's now 0215, and we need to get as close to the water as we can before daylight. Come on, men. Let's go."

We loaded back into the truck as comfortably as possible and pulled back onto the road. Kwan drove on for a couple of hours, turning left and right several times. "I hope you know where you're going. What are you doing, looking for an old girlfriend's house?" said Grayson, but Kwan couldn't hear him from the back. We had met several other vehicles on the road, but there were no new incidents. In about twenty or thirty minutes, as we were approaching another village, he slowed down and eased off the road again, hiding in the trees.

He turned off the engine and said to us, "We will not be able to get to the inlet tonight. It will be daylight soon, and this is a good place to stop. Besides, one of our contacts lives just up the road from here. I will go find him. Rho will stay here until I return."

Gunny replied, "Sounds good, Sergeant. We'll hold right here. Be careful."

Kwan left his rifle in the truck but double-checked his pistol before he left. He walked on through the trees and was soon out of sight.

"Okay, men," said the major with his usual greeting. "Find a comfortable spot and eat your choice of rations [as if we had a choice of rations] and get as much rest as you can until Kwan gets back. Gunny, set the watch with two men and everyone else get some rest. I'm going to lie down for a few minutes myself." Major Gordon was asleep in two minutes.

I checked on Duncan's wound and changed the bandage, so I could take a little better look at it. It looked clean as best I could tell from the dim light of my flashlight. I gave everyone the lecture on dry socks and foot powder and got the same kidding back. I guess I was just everyone's "mother," according to what I heard back from them. The rations tasted pretty good, but a cup of hot coffee would have been a lot better.

Just after 0900, Kwan and two Koreans came back to our encampment. Kwan introduced his friends to us. They were carrying three sacks that they set down in front of us. Kwan opened them and handed each of us small loaves of fresh bread and hunks of cooked pork. That woke us all really quickly. There was plenty to go around. They also had a jug of herbal tea that was unbelievable. Kwan told us, "This will make you feel better. My grandmother fixed this tea for us everyday for young and old alike." We thanked them for the food. It was a feast for all of us, and we were most appreciative.

The major shook hands with the Koreans and spoke to them in their own language. They talked for a half hour, laughing at times and talking seriously about our situation. One of the Koreans kept pointing to the west and making wave motions with his hands.

Rho was sitting with us and filling us in on the conversation. They would accompany us to the inlet across from Nampo where he had a fishing boat and then take us out into Korea Bay. From there, we'd sail on down into the Yellow Sea and into Kanghwa Bay, landing us in South Korea.

"Okay, men," said the major, "We'll stay here until 2200 tonight, and our friends will take us to the sea, where we'll get a ride on a fishing boat. A couple of you have expressed disappointment that we did not find and rescue any of the prisoners. Let me assure you, we did everything humanly possible, but they had been moved and we had no way to get to them. You have sufficient accomplishments to declare this a very successful mission. So far, we have been fortunate and everything has gone better than might have been expected. Now, get some rest. God knows, you've earned it."

"Sir, I have a question," I said.

"Now why does that not surprise me, Doc!" he quipped.

"I know there are some things we don't talk about, but where in hell did you learn to communicate with the Koreans so fluently?"

He looked around seriously and said, "I was wondering how long it would take you to ask that. All of you now know about my background. When I was a child, my dad was stationed in Japan; we had a Korean nanny who taught us her language and also tutored us in our studies. I can also carry on conversations in Japanese. To completely fill you in—when we were stationed in Germany and then France, guess what? Yep, I can also converse in German and French. I'm not just an old dumb navy brat that you have me pictured as. Now shut up and get some sleep. That's all, Doc!" he laughed, making a sound like Bugs Bunny. He surprised us everyday.

Of course, I had to end the conversation with, "Imagine that, a sense of humor, too." No one laughed, but I did get a smile from the major.

I took my turn on watch from 1200 to 1600 with Duncan. His arm was sore, but he was going to be okay. We were relieved by Grayson and Reeves. We went back over and found a spot under the truck to take another nap.

At 2130, we started getting to our feet. "Get your gear together, check your weapons, and get everything onto the truck," said Gunny. "We'll be a little crowded with two more, but make the most of it. Kwan, where are our new friends? It's about time to get out of here."

"They'll be back on time. Maybe they'll bring some more bread and roasted pork. As a matter of fact, here they come now," said Kwan. And yes, they did have some more food to take with us on the trip back.

"Load 'em up," said Major Gordon. "Check the area and don't leave anything behind. Give me a count before we get on the road, Gunny."

Gunny was the last one onto the truck and called out, "Thirteen accounted for, Major. Move it out, Kwan." We pulled out onto the road, and everyone was ready to go.

We rode on up the road for an hour, when Kwan started slowing down. "There's a checkpoint up ahead, Major, but I can't stop or they will become suspicious."

"Move on up slowly and stop if they ask you to. We will stay down out of site as long as possible."

"Okay, Major. There are two jeeps, one on either side of the road. There are five men with automatic weapons, but they are slung on their shoulders, not at the ready."

"Move slowly," said the major, "keep your heads down, men, but be on the ready on each side." The truck came to a stop. Kwan spoke to them, and they pointed to the back of the truck.

"Now," yelled the major. "Fire, fire!" We stuck our rifles out each side of the truck from under the flaps and started firing, taking them by surprise. One of the soldiers got off one burst, but that was it.

"Get out of here, Kwan!" yelled Major Gordon. "Keep it moving as fast as we can go and not wreck this thing!"

We sat back down, looked around, and Potter punched me, "Doc, take a look at those two." He pointed over to two men lying face down on the floor. I grabbed Holder by the arm and pulled him over onto his back. There were two bullet wounds in his chest and one beside his nose. There was no pulse at all—he was gone.

"Holder is dead, Gunny, no question about it," I said. I then reached over and turned Reeves over, and he tried to sit up. "Don't move, Ed," I told him. "Just relax and let me see where you're hurt." He had a wound in his upper right chest, and it also looked like a bullet nipped the top of his ear. Three or four were holding their flashlights over for me to see.

"Just like the last one," he said.

"Well, not as bad this time, Ed. This one is above your lung, and you're going to be okay." I was applying a pressure bandage while I felt around his back. "Ryan, get a morphine syringe here and give him a shot. I'm holding this bandage, but I can't find an exit wound in his back." I ripped his jacket off and got down to bare skin. He was hit just under his collarbone, and we could not find the exit wound. "The bullet is still in his shoulder. Major, we need to stop somewhere, so we can treat him. I need to find that round and get it out, if I can. He doesn't seem to be bleeding too badly. I'll keep pressure on this, and I've got to keep him from going into shock. He's already passed out. Hand me a poncho from under the seats." Two or three handed me ponchos, and we got Ed covered to keep him warm. I took another poncho and put it over Holder to respect his privacy. "We'll get his dog tags when we get him back to base."

We moved on down the road for another thirty minutes until we came to a crossroads. Kwan turned right and found a good place to conceal our truck so we could work on Reeves. I got him up on a seat lying on his back. "Give me some light, guys." Four of them held lights on Reeves's chest. I moved one light right over the wound and started probing with my forceps. "Nothing," I said at first. "It did not go straight back. The bullet probably hit his scapula and deflected downward. I'll have to pack the wound and bandage it." I couldn't find the bullet, so we would have to get him to a hospital as soon as possible. After I bandaged his chest, I immobilized his right arm across his stomach and pulled a jacket around his shoulders and buttoned it in front.

Reeves opened his eyes and looked around. "What happened?" he asked. "Why am I tied down?"

I patted him on the arm. "Take it easy, Ed," I said. "You got shot in the chest again, but at least this one didn't go through your lung. Looks like another trip to Yokosuka for you." He looked around and asked if everyone else was all right. "We're doing just fine. Are you in any pain? We'll keep you as comfortable as possible." He winced a little as he tried to move, so I gave him another shot of morphine. He was back asleep again in a couple of minutes.

"It's after midnight, so we better start moving if we're going to catch that boat," said the major. "Rho, are you going to drive awhile? Okay, you and Kwan keep us on the right path, and let's get moving. Try not to find another checkpoint. We've had too much excitement for one day."

We stopped for a break around 0300 on a quiet coastal road. The truck was rolling again in ten minutes. Reeves was still sleeping, and his pulse and respirations were still good. At 0450, we pulled slowly into a sleeping village. Rho drove around through the streets and stopped at the docks where ten or more fishing boats were tied up. "This is it," said Kwan. "Everyone get your gear off the truck. Let's get Reeves and Holder aboard the boat. Let's get ready to board the fishing boat." After the truck was unloaded, one of the Koreans backed it out and moved it around behind the houses. Kwan said, "The truck will be moved far away from this village before noon today."

Our Korean friends got us situated under a covered area of the boat and cast off. They pushed us away from the dock and out into the stream, heading out into Korea Bay. One of the sails was soon raised, and it pulled us along slowly. After a while, we were out into deeper water, and they raised another sail. Our speed picked up considerably. We were moving along at a pretty good pace for such a small boat. We soon learned that the boat was merely constructed to look like a fishing boat but was designed to carry cargo in disguise. It reminded me of the old "rum runner" skiffs of the 1920s and '30s during the prohibition days of America. The speed of the boat made us feel a little better about our chances of getting back to South Korea.

We were brought out on the deck four or five times during the day. The air felt good rustling through our hair. Reeves was sitting up some. I gave him water several times, and I got him to eat a little of the bread, but he couldn't handle anything else. I got him to take two APCs on two occasions. I was worried he would get an infection, but I had taken all the precautions available to me.

We rocked along throughout the day, and after dark, we saw the sails coming down. We were approaching land. We glided into an inlet and slid right up to a lighted dock. There were U S marines there waiting for us. Semper Fi!

Edwards and I carried Reeves up to the gunwale and handed him up to the marines. "He needs to get to the hospital as soon as possible. He has a bullet in his right shoulder and needs immediate attention," I told them.

"Doc, you go on with them, and we will bring your gear," said the major. We will find out where you are. We'll take care of Holder; don't worry about anything else."

We followed the marines on up the dock to the navy ambulance. We got Reeves on a stretcher and into the ambulance, and took off to the nearest doctors. Twenty minutes later, we pulled up to a tent hospital near a small airstrip. There were two doctors waiting when we carried Reeves in.

"He was shot in the right shoulder, sir," I said to the doctor tending to Ed. "The bullet went in just below the clavicle and hit the scapula and turned downward. I could not locate the round. A round also tipped his right ear, but that's okay for now. As far as I could determine, those are his only wounds, but that's enough."

The doctor patted me on the shoulder, "You've done a great job, corpsman. We'll take him from here." The two corpsmen on duty took Ed into the treatment room, and the two doctors went to work on him. I sat down in one of the padded desk chairs to wait for them to take care of Reeves.

I went to sleep in no time. I woke up after about an hour with my head on the desk. When I sat up, one of the corpsmen came over. "You need to get back to your unit and get some rest. Why don't you come over to our mess tent and get some breakfast? I'll go with you."

"That sounds good to me," I said. "But, how is Reeves? Where is he now?"

"Your patient is still in surgery, but they are about through," said the corpsman. "They removed the bullet,- and he is doing great. We'll have him up and going in a day or two. He will probably go to Seoul today and be flown to Yokosuka Naval Hospital within twenty-four hours. Now, let's go eat breakfast."

After a large breakfast and four cups of coffee, we went back to the tent hospital. I went in and was able to see Corporal Reeves. He was a little groggy but recognized me. "Hey, Doc," he said, "I've done it again. I hope this one doesn't take as long to get over as that last one."

I laughed at him saying, "I know it, Ed. We've just got to find another form of recreation. This kind of fun just seems to get us down."

The doctor came out and put his hand on my shoulder asking, "Has anyone taken a look at you, corpsman?"

I backed away saying, "I'm okay, sir. This isn't my blood," as I looked down at my dirty, soiled fatigues. "All I need is a good hot shower, clean clothing, and a good night's sleep."

The marine standing by the door, a lance corporal, said, "That is what I'm here for, Doc. I'm here to take you up to Munsan Airstrip to join your recon team. They are waiting on you now."

I turned around and shook hands with Reeves and said, "I've got to go now, Ed, but I'll see you in Yokosuka."

He waved as we started for the door, "Thanks for saving my butt again, Doc." I threw up my hand as we went out the door.

"He's a good marine," I said as we went over to the jeep. "He has to be." said the lance corporal. "I'm in training to join Recon. I may be with you on the next trip out."

I looked over to him saying, "Good luck, Lance Corporal. I hope you make it, but I won't be going on the next trip. This was my last one!"

Of course, I was asleep when we arrived at Munsan. "Here we are, Doc," said the driver. "Over here is your tent. Good luck."

I got out of the jeep and said, "Thanks for driving me up here, Corporal. And good luck to you with the Recon Team."

I went into the tent and there sat the major, Gunny, and Ryan. "There you are, Doc. How is Corporal Reeves doing?" As I took off my belt with two med packs, my canteen, and the .45 pistol and dropped it to the floor, I said, "Reeves is great. They got the bullet out, and he's on his way to Seoul and will be flown to Yokosuka. He said to tell you he is doing great and will be back before long."

"Now that you are here, we've gotten everything taken care of. We had Holder taken to Seoul already and have already done his paperwork. You don't have to worry about any of that. Let's get to our barracks down in Seoul, and we can get cleaned up. I want to get the debriefing taken care of today also. It'll be after 1300 before we get down there. Round everyone up, Ryan, and we'll move out. Grab your gear and let's go." We went out to the bus and took a seat.

We were about two miles into the trip when the major stood up and headed to the back of the bus laughing. He pulled a cooler out and set it down in the middle of the aisle. "There you go, guys. The beer is on me this time. Someone grab that box of sandwiches off the back seat. There should be some pepperoni in there, too." The major grabbed the first bottle and popped off the cap and passed the opener around.

Gunny stood up in the aisle, "Here's to our brother, Private Jackson Holder, honored member of the United States Marine Reconnaissance Team."

"Semper Fi," responded everyone to the clink of the glass bottles. We were all finally relaxing and grabbed a sandwich, and Gunny cut the pepperoni sticks into shorter pieces and passed them around.

"I have an announcement," said Gunny. "I have enjoyed thirty-two years in the marine corps, and in two weeks, I'll be an ever-loving stinking civilian. I'm fifty-two years old, and I am going to have to learn to work for a living." A big cheer went up, and another toast was given to the gunny.

"You'll never make it, Gunny," said Ryan. "You'll punch your boss in the mouth the first day." That got a big laugh. We had a fun time all the way back to Seoul.

When we arrived at the base, Major Gordon hustled us into a conference room. "Settle down in here, guys. We're going to get the debriefing over with in short order." He was gone about five minutes and came back in with Captain Blakenship and two of his people. They already had statements typed out for each of us to sign.

"Captain, Corporal Edward Reeves was wounded and is in the hospital here in Seoul awaiting transfer to Yokosuka. You can catch him there. You will not need a statement for Private First Class Jackson Holder. We can all sign our statements now. I've already filled my men in on the procedures."

Captain Blankenship looked around, "I recognize most of you and know that you're aware of the seriousness of revealing information, so be aware of the consequences if you violate these procedures. My men will now pass your respective statements out and witness each signature." This took a half hour because each witness had to explain the statements to each of us.

Captain Blankenship dismissed us and wished us all well. The major led us over to our barracks where we took hot showers and got clean clothing. We went to sleep before dark and had a good night's sleep in a quiet wing of the barracks.

Reveille came at 0600 hours. Major Gordon told us to have a good breakfast and to meet in the conference room at 0800 for his own debriefing session. Gunny went with us to the chow hall, and we spent an hour reminiscing about his military career.

He had joined the marine corps after trying college for one year. "I made pretty good grades, but I just didn't fit in with most of my classmates. I decided to try the military for one term and see what I wanted to do with my life. Even in boot camp at Parris Island, South

Carolina, I knew right away what my career would be. Everyone was honest with me, and I knew where I stood with them. It was tough, but it was all black and white. What you saw was what you got, and if you wanted something, you worked for it. I saw combat in the Second World War in the South Pacific in all the rough places. I was wounded three times, patched up, and sent right back in the middle of it. I wasn't the only one either; that was the way of life in those days. Things were different in Korea. In WWII, we knew who our enemies were, and combat was head to head. In Korea, half the soldiers didn't wear uniforms, and you couldn't tell the enemy from the civilians. The enemy soldiers took advantage of that by posing as civilians and attacking us when we least expected them to.

"Enough of that. This has been a great run. I've enjoyed serving with you men, and you have made my life easier ... for the most part," he laughed. "Now, let's go see what the major has in store for us, before I say something you can use against me."

Back in the conference room, Major Gordon stood up after we were all seated and got quiet enough for him to be heard. "We had a successful mission but with a tragic loss. Jack Holder was a good marine and apparently had a good career ahead of him. We all salute him and his family. Now, we'll be going on another mission in two months. We cannot give up on those prisoners being held up there, although the North Koreans and Chinese still deny the existence of any POWs. We, of all people, know they're lying dogs.

"As for us, I'll still be in charge of the team. We now know that Gunny is leaving us and escaping *to the other side.* Staff Sergeant Ryan will replace Gunny and no other assignments have been finalized. We know Doc's not coming back, and it's my opinion he'll be bored with duty aboard a ship after the exciting life he led with our team. Corporal Reeves will probably move on to training future team members. He won't go on anymore missions. Some of you have other assignments, so I wish you the best of luck. One more thing—keep in mind your agreement not to divulge any details concerning our missions. Be proud of your time with your Recon Team and what it stands for. Good luck, men. Semper Fi!"

"Semper Fi, sir!" came our reply in unison. It was a good day.

CHAPTER 9

BACK TO SEA—AGAIN

The trip back to Japan to rejoin my ship was as routine as usual. I was flown from Seoul to Tachikawa Air Base and took a military bus to Yokohama. When I checked in at Yokohama, I was told the *Sultan* would not be in port for three weeks. The chief yeoman came over and asked me if I could type. "Yes, sir," I replied. "I'm not the best, but I can type."

He waved his hand back around the office and said, "Choose your desk. We are short by ten people, so you have a job for the next three weeks."

Well, here I go again, volunteering without meaning to, but maybe a paper cut is the worst injury I could receive here.

The three weeks went by rather quickly, but I was bored out of my skull. I stayed in the staff barracks just behind the administrative building and next door to the chow hall, so it really wasn't that bad. I just counted the days until I could get back on my ship.

The day before the *Sultan* came into port, the chief yeoman and the staff went out to dinner with me. I appreciated their thoughtfulness, but they wouldn't miss a chance to go out for few drinks anyway. I had a good time and got back to the barracks early to pack my few belongings and be ready to leave the next morning.

I was waiting on the pier when the *Sultan* docked at 1015 hours. After the dependents disembarked, I finally got a chance to get up the gangplank and make it to my room. No one was there; they must have gone ashore already. I unpacked my few items and went up to the hospital. HM2 Williams was in the office, "Come on in, Gentry. Are you here for a visit or coming back to work for us?"

"Ha, ha," I said, "as if any of you work around here. What's the schedule for this trip?"

"We are out of here at 1000 tomorrow and heading to Manila for two days. We then head back to Fort Mason for four days and right back here again."

And so for life back at sea. The voyage to Manila and then to San Francisco was quiet and uneventful. The weather was clear and sunny on the trip all the way back to the United States. I spent every hour available to me on the deck—by myself most of the time, just reflecting on the past few months and enjoying the sunshine. I could not get my mind off of my friends that had been lost on those past five missions. There was no one to talk to about them, so I just talked to them as if they were with me while soaking up the sunshine and peacefulness. Corpsman Williams was just not someone I could talk to freely, even though he had been on several missions with the recon team. Actually, he was more of a talker than a listener, so I just didn't bother him with it anymore. It was more pleasant to feel the sunshine, watch the horizon where the sea met the sky, and smell the salt air as the wind rustled through my hair.

When we arrived at Fort Mason, we were told we would be there for six days before returning to Japan. I called Lieutenant Martha Donovan at Oakland Naval Hospital and asked her if she and Dr. Noblitz could go to church with me that week. There was an old Mission Church in the Oak Knoll area that I had attended several times when I was hospitalized. They made arrangements for me to stay in the barracks on Saturday night with the corpsmen that I knew.

On Sunday morning, HM2 Scott Lewinsky and I met Lieutenant Donovan and Commander Noblitz at the Mission Church. Martha said the church was well over 200 years old and had been a church for all faiths from its inception. The stucco building had the most beautiful walnut furniture and fixtures I had ever seen. The lights hanging from the hewn wooden beams looked like old lantern chandeliers—though they had been fitted with electric lighting, of course. We walked in and sat on the walnut benches with the thick, cushioned seats of red velvet. It was just like stepping back in time.

Before the service began, I went up front and lit eight candles, one each for Private Dawson, Corporal Mattingly, Private McMartin,

Corporal Park, Corporal Sawkowski, Private Harris, Lieutenant Skinner, and Private Holder. I kneeled in prayer for two or three minutes and looked up when I felt hands on my shoulders. I turned around and there was no one there—at least, not visible to anyone. The sermon that day was entitled "Love Your Fellowman!" I wish every one could have been there.

I made that next trip back to Japan with a feeling of contentment and thankfulness. Nothing bothered me now, and I actually enjoyed working with the crew. It was a good trip with good weather except for a couple days of rain half way to Japan.

We unloaded the troops and dependents on the day we arrived. Stayed overnight and picked up 4,200 more troops and 225 dependents. The *Sultan* headed back to Fort Mason, and I was expecting that to be my last trip. I had just three weeks left on my enlistment. When we docked in San Francisco at Fort Mason, I had my sea bag packed and was ready to go over to Treasure Island Naval Base for my separation from active duty. One of the corpsmen came to the door and said, "Gentry, the chief wants to see you in his office." Okay. That sounded good.

"Hi, Chief Hanes, what's up?" I said.

"Come in and have a seat, Larry," he replied. "I know your enlistment's up in three weeks, but you have been assigned another cruise with us."

No way, I thought. "How did that happen, Chief?"

He laughed, "Maybe it won't be too bad this time. I know you have been pulled in several directions for the last year or two. This cruise is to Honolulu with two days there and then return back here. Then you'll still have a week before you either re-enlist or transfer to Treasure Island for separation."

I laughed at him, "Now I know why you want me on this trip to Hawaii. No, Chief; no offense, but I'm not going to re-enlist, even if you transfer me to Hawaii."

"Actually, this has nothing to do with your enlistment. It's a two-week trip, and you have three weeks left, so it's just good business." I knew what the deal was; I just wanted to give the chief a hard time. I really didn't mind two days in Honolulu.

The trip to Hawaii went great. I was lucky to have the two days in Honolulu and spent one night at the Hilton on the beach. We went over to hear the young Don Ho sing again, but he was not at home then. It is still hard to imagine him as an Air Force fighter pilot! We had a good dinner and enjoyed the music they were playing anyway.

Back in San Francisco, I bade farewell to all my shipmates. I was transferred off the ship to Treasure Island. I was there for eight days—two days after my scheduled separation date, because of a problem with my paperwork. "Doc," one of the yeomen said to me, "you sure did have a mixed-up career. They transferred you all over the place, didn't they?"

"Yes they did," I replied. "They sent me to all the problem areas in case someone needed to be shot." He looked at me real funny but didn't say anything.

They finally completed the process, and I was separated from active duty. I was assigned to the Navy Reserves at the U S Navy Reserve Center in Charleston, South Carolina. That was a long way from my home in North Carolina.

That was quite a run. I was very fortunate to get the education and experience I received in the navy. Many of the friendships have lasted to this day. I don't see them anymore but would love to. We all still have those memories.

After my separation from active service, I visited with several friends and family on my six-week trip driving home to North Carolina from California. I bought a 1952 Chrysler DeSoto in San Lorenzo that drove and rode great. That was probably the last time I would have a chance to see some of my friends.

Choosing not to stay in the medical field, although our family doctor offered to sponsor me as a physician's assistant, I went to business school and got a degree in accounting. I enjoyed a good career in the business world and in government. I was married soon after coming home and our first of four children was born while we were in college. Along the way, I held public office on two levels and enjoyed working in way too many political campaigns. I've enjoyed it all.

One of the many interesting things occurred in the first ten years after I got out of the navy. Once each year following my separation, two men who identified themselves as Secret Service, visited me and questioned whether I had discussed my activities with the Marine Recon Team with anyone at all, including my wife. Sometimes they came by my workplace, and at other times, visited me at my home. I assured them—and I assure you—I never once divulged any information concerning that part of my life during that time. I always introduced them as former military friends who came by for a visit. After the tenth year, I never saw them again. Until now, I have not told many people about those experiences.

I am still very proud to have served as a hospital corpsman. I received my training at the US Hospital Corps School at Great Lakes, Illinois. One of my instructors there was HM3 William R. Charette, who was awarded the Medal of Honor for his actions in Korea while treating the wounded and protecting them from further injury. Corpsman Charette retired from the navy in 1977 as Master Chief Hospital Corpsman. He and the other instructors were such an inspiration, role models to us all.

In the Continental Navy and early United States Navy, medical assistants were chosen at random from the ships' crew for various duties. Back then, in the early 1800s, a trained medical assistant was called a surgeon's steward, and later became known as a bayman. The US Navy Hospital Corps was established by Congress and signed into law by President William McKinley on June 17, 1898. The navy corpsman evolved from the hospital apprentice, in various classes, to the pharmacist's mate, in various classes, and on to the present day hospital corpsman, of course in various classes from hospitalman apprentice through master chief hospital corpsman.

From World War I, World War II, the Korean War, the Vietnam War, and on to the present, hospital corpsmen have served throughout the Navy fleet, hit the beaches with the marines and the deserts and mountains in-country in Iraq and Afghanistan. They serve as ward corpsmen, laboratory technicians, x-ray technicians, operating room technicians, pharmacy technicians, emergency-room specialists, and serve on independent duty in ships, submarines, and remote locations where no doctors are available. The army and the air force also have their own medical assistants that perform duties in support of their medical staff, just as the navy hospital corpsmen serve.

I salute the military medical caregivers in all branches of service whether serving the US Navy and Marine Corps, the US Army, the US Air Force, or the US Coast Guard.

CPSIA information can be obtained at www.ICGtesting.com
233819LV00001B/33/P